Southern cultures

Winter 2007, The Global South
Published by the
University of North Carolina Press
for the
Center for the Study of the American South
at the University of North Carolina at Chapel Hill

Y0-AFQ-488

Essays

front porch

The American South has depended on foreign contacts for centuries, ever since Jamestown started down Tobacco Road. From the earliest colonial days, foreign exports propped up the southern economy, as rice, indigo, deerskins, and finally cotton followed tobacco hogsheads into the holds of trans-Atlantic vessels. The Peculiar Institution itself was a product of the global economy, for what else provided the demand for all those exports, or supplied the labor to grow them? The Confederacy learned a hard lesson in the importance of global connections when federal blockaders proved that cotton could not be king without customers. The

above:

As corporations around the globe today compete to capture China's vast market, Nan Enstad reminds us that southern tobacco targeted that country's consumers and tapped its workforce as early as 1905, in "To Know Tobacco: Southern Identity in China in the Jim Crow Era." Shanghai, a century after the city served as the initial assignment for new southerners who came to work in China for British American Tobacco, courtesy of FC Georgio, Wikimedia Commons, under the GNU Free Documentation License.

lesson sank in again after Reconstruction, when sagging world demand for cotton caused more southern poverty than carpetbaggers ever had. Exports were so important that free trade and low tariffs found a permanent place on the South's agenda in Washington—at least until southern factories started losing their trade wars with China.

Despite the centrality of its international connections, the South has also had a traditional reputation for isolation, and it's not hard to see why. The colonial South was a polyglot place, with inhabitants from all over western Europe, western Africa, and the American Indian nations, but things began to change about 1800. As the plantation system strengthened its grip and spread inland, economic opportunities for free immigrants began to dry up. After 1808 the close of the Atlantic slave trade cut off contact in that direction. By 1850 the South trailed the United States in its proportion of foreign-born residents, and it would keep that status until the 1980s. For most of the twentieth century, immigration stayed so low—and racial discrimination stayed so strong—that the boast of "pure Anglo-Saxon labor" became a proud talking point for industry-hunting boosters throughout the region.

Isolation bred homogeneity. For all their differences, black and white southerners developed a remarkable similarity in speech, food, and religion. Pockets of distinctiveness in the mountains, the Sea Islands, and the Cajun bayous did not disturb the South's powerful reputation for cultural unity. "If it can be said that there are many Souths, the fact remains that there is also one South," W. J. Cash famously declared in his 1940 classic, *The Mind of the South*, and generations of readers nodded in agreement.

Back in the day, even out-of-state people were exotic in most parts of the South. In 1950 Mississippi led the nation in its proportion of residents from that state (88.5 percent), and eight of the top ten states in that category were southern. For most of the twentieth century, thousands of people moved away from the South every year, while very few moved to the South or even from state to state inside it. Most southerners were descended from people who had "always" lived there. Of all parts of the United States, the South had the most immobile population and the weakest links to a world beyond its boundaries.

Today that state of affairs is suddenly as gone with the wind as the world of Scarlett and Ashley. The proportion of foreign-born southerners is now five times higher than it was at the end of World War II. In the 1970s and 1980s, a flood of European and Japanese investment brought scores of foreign companies to the Sun Belt; the collapse of global trade barriers shook the southern economy in the 1990s and afterwards, and a burst of immigration has brought us millions of newcomers from other parts of the United States and around the world. While the South has never been disconnected from the outside, the changes of recent decades have now brought America's most isolated region into closer contact with global influences than at any time in memory.

This edition of *Southern Cultures* is dedicated to exploring those contacts, and it is our biggest issue ever. We have some heavy-hitting essays that document the facts of the situation and some lighter pieces that explore how global connections have changed southern culture, both now and in the past. As a special bonus, we're including a DVD prepared by the Southern Oral History Program documenting the lives of recent immigrants in Durham, North Carolina. As varied as they are, none of our authors can tell the whole story, so we look forward to more global offerings in the future.

Let's start at the end of the issue and the beginning of the story. For many native southerners, nothing says "down home" more authentically than barbecue — and nothing provokes more arguments than the question of which regional recipe is the best. The South has plenty of barbecue experts, but John Shelton Reed has researched the subject so thoroughly that he is about to bring out a book on it. In this excerpt, Reed tells us that barbecue is not a southern invention but an international and cross-cultural import from the West Indies, adopted from the Indians along with corn and succotash. So however it's cooked, this most traditional dish reminds us that southern globalization is a very old process.

Nan Enstad offers another look at an earlier global south by telling us about the men who spread southern tobacco across China at the turn of the twentieth century. They were agents of a giant multinational corporation, the British American Tobacco company, but they got there through their roots in the tobacco-farming culture of North Carolina and Virginia. Bright Belt memories bonded the sales force in a far-off land and made them more effective as they taught their customers how to smoke, grow, and cure tobacco. Like globalized barbecue, the result was another irony: the food and manners of Danville and Rocky Mount were harnessed to a corporate strategy, and a "traditional" southern identity became a technique of international business. In changing times, it's worth remembering that tradition can be a highly flexible quality, and not always what it seems to be.

How did the current wave of globalization get started? We all know parts of the story: falling tariffs, cheap transportation and instantaneous communication, the end of Communism, the Internet. But how did these changes affect particular places and what have they meant for the South? Peter Coclanis and Louis Kyriakoudes have taken a close look at what happened in North Carolina in recent decades and find that globalization has had very different effects in different places. Tar Heel cities have flourished in the new economy, they report, but rural areas have suffered, and not because globalization has injured agriculture. Instead, they tell us, mechanization killed off most agricultural employment in the rural South a generation or two ago, and farm workers turned to the factory and low-wage manufacturing. Now those jobs are disappearing in the face of global competition. With no obvious substitute in sight, North Carolina and similar states are left with flourishing cities, a blighted countryside, and a major challenge for policymakers.

If low-wage, low-skill jobs are vanishing across the South, you might well ask why the South is now attracting so many poorly paid, unskilled immigrants. Answers are complicated, but two of our features have illuminating insights. Carl Bankston's "New People in the New South" tells us that not all immigrants are alike and they are not all going to the same places. The South's thriving cities and suburbs are attracting knowledge workers from all around the world. While they and their well-schooled, native-born colleagues are glued to their computers, they want other people to cut the grass, wash the dishes, roof the houses, kill the chickens. No matter how hard things get for the forty-five-year-old, laid-off textile worker with ailing parents, she is probably not ready for this kind of work, but strong, ambitious young people, who see no better options in Mexico, are eager for the challenge. In her interview with Bill Smith, chef of Chapel Hill's famed Crook's Corner restaurant, Lisa Eveleigh brings us a vivid picture of these immigrant workers and an employer who has welcomed them. Readers who have found the people of the Nuevo New South faceless and puzzling until now will find a warm personal close-up in the stories from Smith's kitchen. Even more, the Southern Oral History Program's DVD, *Neighborhood Voices/Voces del Barrio*, brings us the immigrants' stories directly, explaining how it feels to see the South as part of "El Norte."

Can the South benefit from globalization? John Russell is a native southerner and a top executive of Quintiles Transnational, a contract research company that tests drugs before they are marketed, headquartered in North Carolina's Research Triangle Park. In 2006 Russell spoke at the "Navigating the Global American South" conference at UNC-CH, and we share his remarks in this issue. He tells us about two different approaches to business innovation in a global economy—what he calls "the Institute" and "the Factory"—and he tells us how successful companies use both models to complement each other. Along the way, he tells us why Dixie Belle Textiles still flourishes in the ladies' underwear business, what it's like to be "the Southern Guy," and how C. Vann Woodward can explain why he gets along so well with Russians, Chinese, and South Africans. As a model of business culture in the global South, Russell offers lively and provocative perspective on how we must stay abreast of a changing southern world.

The flood of newcomers in recent years has transformed the southern scene, and three of our features provide dramatically different examples. Tore Olsson takes us to "Your Dekalb Farmers Market" outside Atlanta, which started out as a traditional produce stand and evolved into an immense multicultural emporium offering every conceivable form of fresh food from around the world. Offering a taste of home to Atlanta's myriad immigrants, the market also gives native Georgians a thousand windows into worlds they have never seen. The store's multicultural staff and embracive philosophy offer an inviting glimpse of the international community that is taking shape as the South changes.

A more controversial change is the revival of the ancient sport of cockfighting, which has flourished in the South since colonial days and now enjoys a (mostly illegal) comeback. Marko Maunula takes us to Louisiana, the only southern state where cockfighting remains legal, and finds that the action now attracts a diverse crowd of native whites and blacks and Hispanic immigrants. Far away from the labs and boardrooms that John Russell reports from, Maunula reminds us that cultures are stretching in every corner of southern society as new participants in old games bring people together who would otherwise never meet.

Another example of cultural change appears in our poetry section, "Mason-Dixon Lines." Poet Rebecca Lilly shares poignant images of nostalgic southern landscapes, graced with old homes, pine woods, and shady creeks. Nothing could be more familiar, but how does she do it? With Japanese-style haiku.

How do southerners feel about the global South? In our "South Polls" feature, Larry Griffin and Katherine McFarland take a long, close look at public opinion. Not surprisingly, perhaps, they find that natives of what used to be America's most isolated region are still a bit wary of their newest neighbors. Compared to other Americans, we are more likely to disapprove of recent immigrants or to say that having the right religion is an important qualification for becoming a "real" American. Griffin and McFarland observe that their findings raise "huge questions about both public policy and public morality." Can old southerners learn to accept the new? Or is exclusion still central to "the southern way of life?" From the boardrooms to the grocery stores to the cockpits, the evidence points both ways. As you go through this issue, try some Vietnamese fish sauce on your barbecue and think it over.

Let me close with a word of thanks and welcome. Lisa Eveleigh has served *Southern Cultures* as an outstanding copyeditor since she joined us in 1996. That means that she has been responsible for turning academic prose into something you might want to read. Now Lisa is moving on to coordinate communications for the Center for the Study of the American South. In her place, we welcome Ayse Erginer, our longtime associate editor, to Lisa's old role. We are deeply grateful for all that Lisa has given to *Southern Cultures*, but we are delighted that she can now spread her gifts to the entire Center's work.

HARRY L. WATSON, *Editor*

To Know Tobacco

Southern Identity in China in the Jim Crow Era

by Nan Enstad

Go to one of the tobacco areas in North Carolina or Virginia today and you will still find a large number of people who, as the saying goes, "know tobacco"—people who grew up in close proximity to multiple stages of tobacco's production. A great many tended it on the farm when young, learned to cure it and bring it for sale in the tobacco markets. Some came to cities like Winston-Salem, Durham, Reidsville, Petersburg, or Richmond to work in factories producing cigarettes or other tobacco products. Box making in the T. B. Williams Tobacco Factory, Richmond, Virginia, ca. 1900, courtesy of the Collections of the Library of Congress.

o to one of the tobacco areas in North Carolina or Virginia today and you will still find a large number of people who, as the saying goes, "know tobacco." That is, you will encounter people who grew up in close proximity to multiple stages of tobacco production: a great many tended it on the farm when young, learned to cure it, and then brought it for sale in the tobacco markets. Some came to cities like Winston-Salem, Durham, Reidsville, Petersburg, or Richmond to work in factories producing cigarettes or other tobacco products. Some learned to grade tobacco so they could work in the markets; others became skilled at maintaining cigarette machines. Virtually all had at one time, and maybe over their entire lives, smoked cigarettes or chewed tobacco or both. They know a lot about tobacco: how it grows, when it needs to be hoed, topped, and suckered, and what pests threaten it; what the different types of leaf look and feel like when cured; how much it has brought on the market over the years; how it smells when it is being processed or smoked; how it feels to pull the smoke deeply into the lungs. "Knowing tobacco" was more than the sum of these facts and experiences; it was a shared way of life that formed the weft for southern culture in tobacco regions. Tobacco was their livelihood, and it wove through the fabric of their days.

This way of knowing is passing away now, as the tobacco industry declines in the United States. Its health risks undeniable, smoking no longer seems like a simple pleasure for a regular guy or a glamorous pleasure for a movie star. The "golden weed" has ceased to yield its magic gold for the people of the upper South, though multinational tobacco corporations continue to reap huge profits in overseas markets. But this way of knowing tobacco was prevalent for generations, and it is part of why, when the cigarette industry globalized in the *early* twentieth century, southern identity became central to global capitalism in China. The transnational industry incorporated southern networks when hiring U.S. employees to work in China, and southern identity became a grounding in China for a new transnational business culture. Globalization required new identities and new ways of relating, and one of the greatest resources for building these was deeply held, complex local knowledge, like knowing tobacco.

James A. Thomas was one person who knew tobacco and dedicated his life's work to promoting it globally. He was born on a tobacco farm near Reidsville, North Carolina, in 1862 and spent his life building the transnational tobacco industry, particularly during his nearly twenty-year stint as the head of operations for the China branch of the British American Tobacco company (BAT) beginning in 1905. He hired hundreds of young white men from Virginia and North Carolina to come to China as well, first to market imported cigarettes made largely in the upper South and soon to build a parallel system of production, from growing American seed tobacco in Chinese fields, to curing the leaf, to producing cigarettes, packaging, and advertising. These men gained crucial opportunities that gave them a foothold on middle-class status. Such jobs were stepping stones to business positions at home in tobacco, advertising, or other fields. In addition, some men made a career in China, rising to management or executive positions in BAT.

The southerners who built BAT China occupied a nexus of contradictions in globalization. They gained lucrative and adventurous opportunities in a modern and growing corporate capitalist venture while development of their tobacco-based hometowns largely suffered from the same transition. They built a successful company that directed profits from their labor to the northern United States and England. After 1890 corporate capitalism replaced nineteenth-century proprietary capitalism. Companies owned and managed by local individuals, partnerships, or small groups could not compete with the corporate capitalist model, which divided ownership and management, raised greater amounts of capital through stockholders, reduced risks, and engaged in larger-scale endeavors. The South seemed left behind, or even exploited, by northern capitalists who were gaining in their ability to control national and overseas markets. But southern employees were players in this process, benefiting from new opportunities and influencing the formation of global capitalism. Southern employees of BAT worked for one of the first multinational corporations and one of the most successful in capturing global markets for its products.

The experience of BAT men in China challenges the widespread notion that the Jim Crow era was the one time period when globalization was not a significant factor in the South, as well as the idea that the South was economically and culturally isolated. Historians have, in recent years, explored how pervasively the South has been linked to global economies during slavery and since the Civil Rights Movement. The slave South was a product of the Atlantic market in raw materials and slaves, and the slave-based plantation was a transnational economic institution. Likewise, since the Civil Rights Movement, immigration flows to all areas of the South have increased, even while some industries, notably textiles and cigarettes, have fled to cheaper labor markets in other countries. These global bookends of southern history have dismantled the southern isolation thesis that held for many years, but it still reigns for the Jim Crow era. Evidence appears to support the view of the South as economically and culturally isolated. The chronic underdevelopment of the South is based partially on economic factors persisting from slavery: a poor base of educational and transportation systems due to slave owners' capital investment priorities in slaves and a low industrial-wage scale tied to agricultural labor prices. Furthermore, the Jim Crow system of segregation set up a costly dual system of social services, straining already burdened town budgets. Depressed wages deterred immigration to the region, while the rise of cor-

The American Tobacco Company was owned and controlled by James B. Duke, originally from Durham, North Carolina, but it must be considered a national, rather than a southern, company. Roundly hated by farmers, the ATC monopoly had the power to set prices for tobacco leaf, and it decided to set them very low. Between 1890 and 1911, the words "American Tobacco Company" sounded like "dispossession" to most people who knew tobacco in the upper South. Rollers and bunch-breakers at the Danville, Virginia, branch of the American Tobacco Company, 1911, courtesy of the Collections of the Library of Congress.

porate capitalism expanded the economic advantage of the North, which greatly exceeded the South in capital investment and control of financial exchanges.[1]

As true as these economic facts are, the isolation thesis occludes the upper South's experience of globalization in the Jim Crow era, both at home and overseas. Globalization is not just an economic force exerted from the outside that produces clear cut winners and losers. Rather, it is a set of ventures and relationships that are achieved culturally. Southern identity did not become irrelevant in the context of globalization; instead, being "southern" became a resource for consolidating an overseas community and functioned as a strategy in creating the structures and affiliations of a new global capitalist endeavor. Knowing tobacco, southern foodways, and southern domesticity were all rooted in the South's system of segregation, and all provided a foundation for a global community of southerners in China.

James A. Thomas's career trajectory was itself a product of the South's struggle with economic underdevelopment and the pathway of tobacco's globalization. Born during the Civil War, Thomas's education had been cut short by the need to help his tobacco-farming family make ends meet, which he did by working in a tobacco warehouse in Reidsville as a fourteen-year-old. He subsequently had to compensate for his poor education by attending a four-month business-college course in Poughkeepsie, New York, on borrowed money, in order to become qualified for a position in sales for a tobacco company. He also saw the fragility of the North Carolina tobacco business first hand: he was first employed by Reidsville's A. H. Motley tobacco company in the mid-1880s to market plug tobacco in California and later in the South Seas. He even bought a share in the company, but he lost that job and his investment in 1896 when the American Tobacco Company of New York (ATC) drove Motley out of business. A. H. Motley, R. P. Richardson, S. C. Penn, and a half-dozen other healthy tobacco companies were the economic backbone of Reidsville, and the growing export business in tobacco products was Reidsville's hope for expanding revenues and future growth. By 1903, however, only one company, R. P. Richardson, had survived the tactics of the ATC monopoly that voraciously bought or buried companies all through the region. Thomas worked for the export divisions of two more companies that were subsequently bought by the ATC, and in 1900 he went to work for the ATC itself in Singapore.[2]

The ATC was owned and controlled by James B. Duke, originally from Durham, North Carolina, but it must be considered a national, rather than a southern, company. As good as Duke was to Durham—placing factories there, purchasing additional industries, giving to Trinity College (later Duke University)—he reorganized his father's company, The W. Duke, Sons and Company, to form the ATC and relocated to New York in 1890, and soon controlled tobacco processing and cigarette and plug manufacturing all over the country. Roundly hated by farmers, the ATC monopoly had the power to set prices for tobacco leaf, and it set them very low. Between 1890 and 1911, the words "American Tobacco Company" sounded like "dispossession" to most people who knew tobacco in the upper South. In 1902 Duke formed BAT, a cooperative venture with Imperial Tobacco Co. Ltd. of London to eliminate competition in foreign trade between the two mammoth companies. Duke served as president, and the ATC owned 66 percent of BAT's stock. This venture, headquartered in London with offices in New York, became a leading U.S. presence in foreign trade, along with Standard Oil. BAT soon marketed cigarettes all over the globe, including Asia, Africa, the Middle East, and Latin America.[3] As an executive for BAT, Thomas would be first to acknowledge that he no longer worked for a specifically southern company that channeled profits to his home state, but for one of the largest and most successful multinational corporations in the world. His experience of globalization was part and parcel of the forces that imperiled the continued development of his hometown.

Nevertheless, or perhaps in part because of this, when it came time for Thomas to hire representatives for the China branch of BAT, he tapped local tobacco networks and offered opportunities to white men like himself from the upper South's tobacco regions. "Most of the Far Eastern representatives of the company in the early days were recruited from North Carolina and Virginia," Thomas explained. "There was no rule about this, but as most of the company's men at home came from these two states, they knew where to find assistants who from infancy had cultivated, cured and manufactured tobacco, so that it was a second nature to them." One tobacconist from North Carolina, Irwin Smith, recalled that this created a network of white southerners in China with strong regional ties: "the people out there, if you didn't know their family, you knew where they came from." Sometimes Thomas identified potential employees himself, particularly in the early years, and Thomas's papers contain numerous requests from close and distant acquaintances for employment. Thomas also relied on local tobacco men who themselves were moving through the rapidly shifting business. George Allen of Warrenton, North Carolina, who worked in BAT's New York office, recommended a number of local men, sometimes funding their passage to China from his own pocketbook. A manager of the ATC factory in Durham and leaf dealers in North Carolina's tobacco belt also recommended men for positions.[4]

Choosing men who "knew tobacco" was one way to direct opportunities to an emergent middle class of white men. According to employee Lee Parker from Ahoskie, North Carolina, almost all of the BAT men had been "tobacco farm boys."[5] Generally, these young men came from propertied and somewhat successful families, and some had been to college. Others, however, came from less privileged backgrounds, like Thomas himself. Opportunities were limited for young white men wishing to achieve or maintain middle-class status in this era. Education had been interrupted for so many that college could not serve as the exclusive pathway to BAT jobs. While textiles were just beginning to boom, tobacco's ability to support continued development was limited by precisely these factors of monopolization and globalization that men responded to when they went to China. Thomas and others shaped employment with BAT as a response to both hardship and new opportunities in the upper South's tobacco industry. BAT jobs thus also became one among many ways to perpetuate race privilege through discriminatory employment practices during the Jim Crow era. While hundreds of black men in North Carolina and Virginia also knew tobacco, none received the opportunity to go to China.

"Knowing tobacco" was among Thomas's hiring criteria, but in fact most of the jobs did not require or utilize prior experience. Workers were surprised to discover this, though it was certainly no surprise to Thomas, who had worked overseas since the 1880s. China was so vastly different from the U.S. South that every aspect of the business, from advertising, sales, and distribution, to manufacturing, to farming, had to be renegotiated in order to fit into Chinese culture and draw upon Chinese workers. The most important employees for facilitating this negotiation were the hundreds of Chinese businessmen (called "compradors") hired by BAT, not men from the upper South. Work in sales and factory supervision was particularly dependent on Chinese businessmen, merchants, and supervisors. "I don't think [knowing tobacco] was worth a nickel. I really don't," said Lee Parker, who worked in sales. "Knowing tobacco didn't mean a thing in the world; all [the job entailed] was to promote the sale of our product and that was about it."[6] For the most part, BAT workers in China received on-the-job training for whatever positions they were most needed to fill.

The one job that did directly utilize knowledge of tobacco was introducing American seed tobacco and flu-curing techniques to Chinese farmers. While Chinese farmers had grown tobacco for centuries, the tobacco was not of the appropriate quality for the American-style cigarettes that BAT and other companies had made popular in China. Farmers from North Carolina, particularly, went to China for these purposes, and a North Carolinian, R. H. Gregory, headed up the project. Even in this case, however, the jobs were often supervisory, acting as representatives for the company in distributing seeds and purchasing cured tobacco, rather than purely instructional in nature, and success depended heavily on Chinese employees who spoke the farmers' language. In some cases, men from the upper South who knew how to cure tobacco worked directly with Chinese farmers, but this endeavor lasted only two months of the year; the remaining ten months they worked in sales, where their knowledge was less imperative.[7]

While experience with tobacco in the upper South was of limited utility in performing the actual work, the common background of "knowing tobacco" was very important in another sense: it served to consolidate an overseas business community and facilitate the emergence of a particular structure of global capitalism. From the moment they arrived in China, the young southern BAT workers had to assimilate into a radically new context and become part of a functioning community of "foreigners" — British and American employees of BAT. They also

British American Tobacco jobs became one among many ways to create race privilege through discriminatory employment practices during the Jim Crow era. While hundreds of black men in North Carolina and Virginia also knew tobacco, none received the opportunity to go to China. Pot press operators at the T. B. Williams Tobacco Factory, Richmond, Virginia, ca. 1900, courtesy of the Collections of the Library of Congress.

had to interact with other "foreigners" as well as Chinese businessmen, interpreters, and servants. BAT contracts were for four years, after which time workers got a paid leave to visit home for four months; a successful capitalist venture depended on most workers making a successful transition to their new life. For virtually all of the BAT workers, this was their first time outside of the South, and many had never before left their native state. Their southern identity formed a base of commonality within BAT, but they also changed in the new context. They did so in the company of other southerners, particularly in Shanghai, the location of the company's headquarters.

When new employees arrived in China, they landed first in Shanghai. There they would stay for several weeks in order to acclimate and receive their first assignment, which could be in the Shanghai offices or factories, or could be in another treaty port or in a more remote trade or agricultural region. Unequal treaties gave foreign companies dramatic advantages in China: foreign companies gained the right to build factories freely in treaty ports after 1895, promoted their goods largely free of Chinese-imposed tariffs, and enjoyed extraterritoriality, which meant that employees could not be held to Chinese laws or tried for crimes in Chinese courts. Shanghai epitomized the shift in tactics of overseas expansion in those years: rather than pursue political annexation, business leaders created "deterritorialized arenas" in which they enjoyed economic advantages and cultural prestige. Consequently, the British and American employees of BAT met employees of scores of other companies from many western countries. Most foreigners in Shanghai lived in the International Settlement or the French Concession, areas of the city governed by municipal bodies of foreigners rather than by the Chinese authorities. Shanghai was called the "Paris of the East," and the nightlife and services for foreigners were so developed that the Chinese could seem like the outsiders to young southerners. "We didn't stay [in Shanghai] long but they did take us out and showed us the city and all," said Irwin Smith. "It was just like any other foreign city except the Chinese were there." When BAT employees arrived, they adapted first to the community of foreigners.[8]

In this new, big city most employees were happy to find a culture of tobacco with a distinctly southern cast. The American Club, the Astor Hotel, and numerous nightclubs anchored this culture. North Carolinian C. Stuart Carr reported that at the American Club, "There were always Americans . . . and usually either North Carolinians or Virginians and we got along well together." In addition, many had learned racist views of Chinese people since childhood and were afraid to go into the Chinese city. James Hutchinson stayed within a few blocks of the Astor Hotel while he was in Shanghai. "The slit-eyes of the Chinese looked so sinister," he explained, "and tales of their mysterious ways were still so fresh in mind, that I was squeamish about venturing too far into their midst." When an interviewer asked Virginian John C. Waddell if he "adopted to the culture" in

Shanghai, he replied, "That's right. It made it nice that there were people there that were just like we were—from Virginia and North Carolina. All of the tobacco folks and plenty of the Standard Oil, Texaco, Coca Cola etc folks were from the South."[9] The southern cast of BAT could not make Shanghai seem like North Carolina or Virginia, but it could create a protected setting within a very unfamiliar context. Many stuck very close to the community of foreigners, especially when new to China.

Southern BAT workers reimagined their identities away from home as part of a global capitalist context. BAT workers from the South had in mind that they were going to a more "primitive" and largely non-Christian country, but they also felt that they were joining a grand venture and a very modern company. Hutchinson, who had never been out of North Carolina and was twenty years old when he arrived in China in 1911, had great hopes for joining a company full of opportunities for young men. "I saw visions," he said. "Here was a new world opening up." A young North Carolinian identified as "Bartlett" met Hutchinson's boat and took him to meet Thomas, who gave Hutchinson a pep talk about the opportunities he could have with BAT if he did well. As Hutchinson listened, he envisioned himself a future leader in the global venture: "I tightened my lips and swelled inside like a pouter pigeon, saw myself relentlessly pushing ahead, glancing at figures, giving curt orders, sitting at the head of a long oak table in the London board room briefly outlining strategy to dignified, obsequious directors." Hutchinson was disappointed to find that the work was far less glamorous and the opportunities more rare than the pep talks and his imagination indicated. Still, he had taken the first steps towards identifying with the company and becoming part of its global mission.[10]

At the same time that BAT workers dreamed globally, many found themselves unprepared for daily life in Shanghai, which was, by far, the most cosmopolitan city that they had ever experienced. Indeed, for them, "primitive" and "modern" were not set polarities attributed to East and West respectively, but ideas that had to be negotiated daily. Many southerners from rural areas did not yet have electricity or indoor plumbing in the early twentieth century. Social life was often family based, and young people most often spent leisure time with people who were part of family, church, or neighborhood networks. In Shanghai they encountered more modern amenities and an elaborate public nightlife, full of perfect strangers. BAT, as a modern multinational corporation, had formal events unlike anything most had experienced at home. Lee Parker recalled that he and two young men from Virginia misunderstood when a BAT executive invited them to a dinner that would be "white tie." "We thought he was trying to be funny. We all laughed heartily." But when the executive came to pick them up, he would not take them without formal attire. "We ate a lonesome meal in the hotel dining room," said Parker. Parker subsequently ordered formal clothes from C. R. Boone, Clothier of

Turn-of-the-century China was so vastly different from the U.S. South that every aspect of the business, from advertising, sales and distribution, to manufacturing, to farming, had to be renegotiated in order to fit into Chinese culture and draw upon Chinese workers. At a street fountain in Shanghai, China, 1901, courtesy of the Collections of the Library of Congress.

Raleigh. "This [requirement] seemed very strange to me," said Parker, "in what I had thought of as a backward country." Young BAT men developed a more "modern" southern identity to facilitate their transition. Perhaps this explains why BAT workers often claimed they came from New South cities rather than small towns. "There was some rivalry among them . . . as to the places from which they came," recalled Thomas.

> Each insisted that he was from one of the larger towns in his state. Once when this subject was being discussed, one young North Carolinian asked another from what town he came. "Durham," the second boy replied. However, after some urging, he admitted that his birthplace was Rock Horse Creek. . . . It was a peculiar thing that most of the boys claimed to come from big towns, though, as a matter of fact, most of them grew up in a small town, which I shall call *Dullsboro.* But what difference, so long as they came from North Carolina or Virginia!

BAT workers forged new, global identities within their relationships with other southerners. Being "southern" was not quite the same in Shanghai as in Rock Horse Creek, but that made it no less crucial to the construction of BAT.[11]

Being southern was also re-created in China through the meals that southerners put on for other BAT workers in Shanghai. Those permanently residing in Shanghai, particularly high-ranking executives, vied to create meals that most resembled the food at home. These gatherings became respites for men recently arrived from "home" or back in Shanghai between assignments. Perhaps it is natural to crave the foods from home when in a foreign environment. "Out in China, when I thought of North Carolina," remarked Thomas, "I would have been willing to pay any price within my limited means for corn bread, salt herring, and black-eyed peas, the food I was accustomed to eat at home. Later on I brought these out with me." Indeed, Thomas's papers document his efforts to ship many different southern foods, including Smithfield Hams, to Shanghai. Hattie Gregory moved to Shanghai in 1912, shortly after her wedding to R. H. Gregory, and immediately set about creating meals that she and her husband might have had in their hometown of Tarboro, North Carolina. The Gregorys' house became a regular stopping point for young southerners and remained so for two decades. When an interviewer asked Irwin Smith if he found Shanghai overwhelming when he arrived in the early 1930s, he said, "Well, you know Mr. RH Gregory, he was out there. He always thought a lot of the young fellows. If you were in Shanghai . . . you were always invited out to his house for Sunday morning breakfast about eleven o'clock." Even when returning stateside, southern meals characterized the BAT experience. When BAT employees traveled through New York City, they found themselves embraced by Allen, the BAT executive who had recommended some of them for employment. Thomas reported, "One of the most loyal friends of our men in the East was Mr. George Garland Allen, a North Carolinian, whose work for the company took him to New York. Mr. Allen helped us very much. He was always optimistic, met us at the wharf when we returned home, took us to his house, and fed us dishes that we had enjoyed when we were boys in North Carolina." Southern meals built on common experiences and tastes to create new affiliations and loyalties as men traversed the globe.[12]

The significance of white women to this process was greater than their numbers, and is often erased in the remembrances of BAT employees who attributed hospitality entirely to the male head of household. While women were not eligible for jobs with BAT, some traveled to China as wives of long-term employees. There they set up households that transplanted many southern practices, particularly ensuring that Chinese servants provided familiar southern meals to their families and to the BAT community. Women went to great lengths to procure ingredients and to teach Chinese cooks to prepare southern dishes. Soon after setting up her home in China, Gregory wrote home to her cousin Kate asking for recipes: "By the way, please write out for me some simple receipts for everyday N.C. and southern dishes—waffles, battercakes, both kinds of egg bread, corn meal and flour muffins, molasses pudding, smothered chicken, etc., anything you think of that we have at home." Gregory was sometimes unsure of how to teach her cook, since she herself had never made these dishes: in North Carolina, an African American domestic worker had made her family's meals. Accordingly, she asked Kate to be detailed in her instructions: "I have a general idea how they are made, and think I could make them myself after a few trials, but it is so much better to have reliable and explicit directions to give these Chinese cooks for a new dish."[13]

The work of southern women and Chinese servants grounded the BAT community in Shanghai in southern foodways. Gregory responded to a friendly competition between the homes of BAT southerners to come up with southern fare. She regularly reported on the menus of dinners at other homes, and she reveled in an entertaining success. She reported home that she had succeeded in teaching the cook to make beaten biscuits, "which are something that I have not eaten at any other house." She also held "a stew"—a Brunswick stew dinner, which was a tradition in North Carolina. She wrote home: "[O]ur Brunswick stew dinner was quite a success . . . Mr. Covington [a BAT executive from Danville, Virginia] came out and showed the cook how to make it. I went out and looked on, so now I am sure that I can make one, or have it made, equally as good." Gregory's daughter Jane recalled that they always ate North Carolina food at home, including barbecue, and never Chinese food. Despite the hundreds of Chinese restaurants in Shanghai, Jane said, "I can't remember eating in a Chinese restaurant, ever."[14] When Gregory taught her cooks to make southern recipes she asked them to take on the social role and physical actions of African American servants at home.

Race was a central component of southern identity in the United States during this period of Jim Crow segregation and modernization, and it remained so for southerners in China. While "southern" could literally describe anyone who lived in the former Confederate states, in fact whites had a stronger claim on the term and, in this period, elaborated a new ideal of a "southern way of life" based on white privilege, black servitude, and segregation. Historian Edward Ayers has argued that segregation was "not a throwback to old-fashioned racism," but in its capacity to rationally order the movement of the races through public space it "became, to whites, a badge of sophisticated, modern, managed race relations." This vision extended to the home and shaped the ideal of domestic service. As historian Grace Hale has argued, black women's domestic service made it possible for working- and middle-class white women to be "new women"—workers and reformers in the public sphere—without sacrificing a notion of domesticity that lay at the core of southern society.[15] In addition, as the home became more of a place of consumption than a place of production, white women's role within it shifted from household producer to household manager of purchase and service. Thus, white women constructed roles and identities in direct relationship to African American women's position in the home. Gregory, then, was likely seen as an adventurous New Woman to go to China as a young bride, and she set up a particularly *southern* home there based on servant labor and organized along very modern ideals forged within southern segregation.

Gregory drew on her experience in the South in asserting her new role as

When new employees arrived in China, they landed first in Shanghai, which was the location of the company's China headquarters. Shanghai was, by far, the most cosmopolitan city that they had ever experienced. Many southerners from rural areas did not yet have electricity or indoor plumbing in the early twentieth century. Social life was often family based, and young people most often encountered people who were part of family, church, or neighborhood networks. In Shanghai, they encountered more modern amenities, and an elaborate public nightlife, full of perfect strangers. Shanghai, ca. 1900, courtesy of the Collections of the Library of Congress.

household manager of a much larger group of servants than her family could have afforded at home, typically four to seven per bat household. As C. Stuart Carr said, "Nobody worked very hard. Everybody had plenty of servants . . . number one boy and number two boy and a cook and a gardener. You name it, they had it. The exchange rate was so favorable. You could have anything that you wanted. It was a glamorous life." What was ease for Carr produced work for Gregory. "Sometimes I feel almost overwhelmed with the number of servants that I have," she remarked. "A boy, cook, coolie, two amahs, in addition to the gardener and the washman, but it is necessary to have them all. . . . I have a very good amah and am satisfied to leave her to do almost everything for the baby." In fact, Gregory initially encountered great difficulty in asserting her role as household manager, for her husband's head servant, called the "number one boy," had held that role. Gregory's daughter recalled, "Soon after she arrived, the number one boy went to her husband and said, He said that 'everything fine,' I 'like everything' but 'I can no stand missy.' He resigned. A number of others also left." Gregory drew directly on her skills as a manager of African American domestic workers in asserting her authority, even coming to see African Americans and Chinese people as inherently similar. She wrote home: "The Chinese are better servants than the negroes, but very much like them in many ways. To get the simplest thing done properly it is necessary to stand right by and watch them—certainly until they get your ideas into their head. As with the negroes, too, it is very necessary to show them that you are the mistress; but once let them understand that and you can get anything done if you know yourself how it ought to be done." North Carolinian Clyde Gore also read Chinese people through the scripted interactions between whites and blacks in the Jim Crow South: "If they like you, they are like the black man here. They will die for you. If they don't like you, they will have nothing to do with you."[16] Southern BAT workers not only interpreted China in terms of the biracialism of the South, they utilized Jim Crow segregation as a template to create the new hierarchies at the foundation of twentieth century global capitalism.

As Gregory's experience showed, Chinese servants found many ways to subvert the authority of their employers. Indeed, their power was accentuated by their knowledge of local conventions and their employers' dependence on their language and cultural skills. Conventions regarding servants' rights and duties were well established in Chinese households as well as within foreign households in the treaty ports. In order to promote their expectations and desires, employers had to negotiate with savvy Chinese servants. For example, when the head servant bought food and supplies for the household, he typically added a surcharge for his own profit; Gregory and other employers had no choice but to accept this surcharge as customary because they did not have sufficient language and cultural skills to do the bartering required for shopping themselves. In addition, while African American domestics in this period largely refused to live-in, asserting their right to maintain their own families and households, a Chinese number one boy asserted his right to move his entire family into servants' quarters in the house, and his employer was often expected to provide his wife with employment as well.

Still, Gregory found something familiar in her relationships with Chinese servants. Her daughter recalled that her mother "told me that there were similarities between dealing with Chinese servants and Negro domestic help back home. She thought that Americans from the South sometimes had an easier time in such relationships than Americans from other parts of the United States. Southerners were accustomed to dealing with servants, people who were in and out of their houses."[17] Thus, BAT homes in China accommodated vast differences from life in the United States but retained a racial definition based on servitude that was discernibly southern.

Young men from the South who went to China as new BAT employees, then, did not lose their southern identity in the context of global capitalism. If anything, being from North Carolina or Virginia took on invigorated meaning in China. Their opportunities emerged from local networks of men who knew tobacco and served to construct race privilege and secure middle-class status for a small but significant group in the New South. These men encountered others, "just like we were," and used this construction of sameness to navigate a new, large company and country. They found particular refuge in southern homes maintained by permanent residents of Shanghai, homes that served up familiar foods and were based on southern domesticity. Though much of their experience in China was startlingly new, southern identity became a resource in constituting a business culture, and thereby helped to construct a particular form of global capitalism. This did not give them power to dictate BAT's activities; none—including Thomas—issued curt orders to obsequious directors in London. Rather, for good or ill, it enabled BAT China to function and gave shared meaning to employees' actions beyond individual profit-seeking. Understanding more about their experiences illuminates the impact of globalization on the South.

Southerners who built BAT China set in motion a history that continues to reverberate to the present. They sparked a dramatic rise in cigarette smoking in China, from less than a third of a billion cigarettes in 1900 to forty billion in 1924. This fueled exports in tobacco leaf and manufactured cigarettes from the upper South, as well as spurred BAT to develop tobacco farms and cigarette factories in China. Chinese companies arose to capture a portion of the burgeoning market. Cigarette smoking in the United States likewise boomed during the 1920s. Tobacco, indeed, seemed to be a golden weed as well as a global obsession.

There were hidden costs, however. The formation of corporations and monopolies at the turn of the twentieth century drastically reduced the number of southern-owned tobacco businesses. New corporations like ATC and BAT utilized southern knowledge but directed profits largely to New York and London. While a handful of towns in the upper South gained huge cigarette factories, scores of smaller, nineteenth-century tobacco towns experienced decline. In addition, even as the global tobacco industry boomed, BAT's dependence on the upper South slowly diminished, and today the historic tobacco links between China and the upper South are largely unknown. Both China and the upper South certainly gained jobs and infrastructure development from the cigarette industry, but in both instances corporations demonstrated more loyalty to distant stockholders than to the health of local economies or human bodies.

Nowhere has this been more obvious than in the tobacco corporations' responses to the public health disaster caused by cigarettes. Even after the dangers of smoking were scientifically proven, tobacco companies obfuscated those findings with cynical public-relations campaigns designed to undermine medical authorities. As markets declined in the United States and Western Europe, tobacco corporations focused more heavily on overseas markets where smoking rates continue to rise. By 2030, 70 percent of all smoking-related deaths will occur in so-called "developing" nations, creating a global public-health disaster of pandemic proportions. In China alone, one hundred million men now under the age of twenty-nine will die from smoking-related causes. Tobacco companies, bolstered by General Agreement on Tariffs and Trade and the World Trade Organization, have successfully utilized the banner of "free trade" to force open markets in poorer countries with less developed tobacco public-health campaigns.[18] People with smoking-related illnesses the world over, including in the upper South, experience globalization on the most personal level. In 1928 Thomas wrote, "No one, perhaps, can ever realize the thrill I received in this work. I felt that I was building a structure that went straight back to my native state, one that would help the farmer there." But from the day he arrived in 1905, Thomas worked to build a parallel production process that would replace U.S. exports with tobacco leaf and manufactured cigarettes produced in China.

The experiences of southerners in China, however, remind us that globalization is not just large economic forces imposed by huge companies but is built out of local resources and achieved through human interactions, that is, through culture. "Local" and "global," for southerners in China as for those who stayed home, were not polar opposites but interrelated and mutually defining aspects of experience. It is important to see the Jim Crow South as part of a long history of the region's engagement with globalization rather than as isolated or parochial, for only in this way can we understand the impact the South had on the nation and the world. Despite its economic disadvantages in relation to the North, "southern" identity performed powerful work during this era. The South asserted a strong influence on U.S. culture in general, a fact abundantly clear in popular national advertising campaigns that celebrated African American servitude, such as those for Aunt Jemima Pancakes and Uncle Ben's Rice. Southern identity, inextricably tied to the modernization project of Jim Crow, was hardly an exclusively regional interest but was in dynamic dialogue with both American identity and global capitalist formations. Today, the upper South's tobacco economy is in steep decline while companies continue to make huge profits on cigarettes in overseas markets. An identity based on knowing tobacco is ever less possible in the upper South. But the globalization of cigarettes that recently cut the U.S. South out of the loop began long ago. It is a story not just about London and New York corporate directors but also about the people of Reidsville, Durham, Danville, Oxford, Winston-Salem, Petersburg, and the rural places in between and how they brought global and local together in their daily lives, staying home or traveling far.

Southern identity, so much a part of the modernizing South, was central to creating global identities and the web of relationships that would constitute global capitalism. The imaginative process of creating oneself as a southerner in a global company was crucial to the cultural production of capitalism in BAT. Southern identity did not wither away in the context of globalization. This story can remind us that southern identity does not spring organically from the soil, a product simply of a long, internalized history, but gains its vitality from living social relations. That is, southern identity performs some work—of modernization, of

Hattie Gregory came to see African Americans and Chinese people as inherently similar. "The Chinese are better servants than the negroes," she wrote, "but very much like them in many ways. To get the simplest thing done properly it is necessary to stand right by and watch them—certainly until they get your ideas into their head." Chinese women weeding the lawn of wealthy foreigners in Shanghai, ca. 1900, courtesy of the collections of the Library of Congress.

globalization, of racialization—and that work has shifted and changed over time and place. Indeed, southerners in China demonstrate that southern identity is not even just about being in the South, and maybe it never was. As the South changes again in our own time through factory flight and immigration, southern identity becomes newly available for work, appropriation, and change. Freighted with hierarchies and hurts, it is unclear who will find it of use and for what purposes, but we might prepare to be surprised.

NOTES

1. A recent iteration of this view may be found in James L. Peacock, Harry L. Watson, and Carrie R. Matthews, eds., *The American South in a Global World* (University of North Carolina Press, 2005).

2. Thomas's life history is drawn from James A. Thomas, *A Pioneer Tobacco Merchant in the Orient* (Duke University Press, 1928); James A. Thomas, *Trailing Trade a Million Miles* (Duke University Press, 1931); James A. Thomas Papers, Perkins Library, Duke University.

3. Howard Cox, *The Global Cigarette: Origins and Evolution of British American Tobacco, 1880–1945* (Oxford University Press, 2000).

4. Thomas, *A Pioneer Tobacco Merchant*, 85–86; Irwin Smith Oral History, 28 July 1982, East Carolina Manuscript Collection, J. Y. Joyner Library, East Carolina University.

5. Lee Parker Oral History, June 1980, East Carolina Manuscript Collection, J. Y. Joyner Library, East Carolina University.

6. Parker Oral History; see Sherman Cochran, *Big Business in China: Sino-foreign Rivalry in the Cigarette Industry, 1890–1930* (Harvard University Press, 1980) for extended discussions of the importance of BAT's Chinese employees.

7. R. H. Gregory to Jeffries, 7 December 1915, James A. Thomas Papers, Duke University.

8. See Amy Kaplan, *The Anarchy of Empire in the Making of U.S. Culture* (Harvard University Press, 2002), 15; on treaty ports see Cochran, *Big Business in China*, 2, 40; Smith Oral History.

9. Carr worked for the Carolina Leaf Tobacco Company and Waddell worked for the Universal Leaf Tobacco Company. Both of these were upper South companies that sold American leaf to manufacturers in China. They both socialized extensively with BAT employees. C. Stuart Carr Oral History, 15 September 1980, East Carolina Manuscript Collection, J. Y. Joyner Library, East Carolina University; James Lafayette Hutchinson, *China Hand* (Lothrop, Lee and Shepard Co., 1936), 14; John C. Waddell Oral History, 15 September 1980, East Carolina Manuscript Collection, J. Y. Joyner Library, East Carolina University.

10. Hutchinson, *China Hand*, 5, 12–13.

11. Lee Parker and Ruth Dorval Jones, *China and the Golden Weed* (Herald Publishing Company, 1976), 14–15, 29; Thomas, *Pioneer Tobacco Merchant*, 85–86, emphasis in original.

12. Thomas, *Pioneer Tobacco Merchant*, 78–79, 308–9; Thomas to E. S. Bowling, 26 October 1915, Thomas Papers; Smith Oral History.

13. Hattie Gregory to Kate Arrington, 13 February 1913, Hattie Gregory Papers, East Carolina Manuscript Collection, J. Y. Joyner Library, East Carolina University.

14. Gregory to Arrington, 14 April 1913, Gregory to Arrington, 19 May 1913, Hattie Gregory Papers; Jane Gregory Murrow Oral History, 1 June 1980, East Carolina Manuscript Collection, J. Y. Joyner Library, East Carolina University.

15. Edward L. Ayers, *Southern Crossing: A History of the American South, 1877–1906* (Oxford University Press, 1998), viii, 100; Grace Elizabeth Hale, *Making Whiteness: The Culture of Segregation in the South, 1890–1940* (Random House, 1998), 106.

16. Carr Oral History; Gregory to Arrington, 7 September 1913, Hattie Gregory Papers; Murrow Oral History; Gregory to Arrington, 13 February 1913, Hattie Gregory Papers; Clyde Gore Oral History, 28 April 1977, East Carolina Manuscript Collection, J. Y. Joyner Library, East Carolina University.

17. Murrow Oral History.

18. Cochran, *Big Business in China*, 234; Allan M. Brandt, *The Cigarette Century: The Rise, Fall and Deadly Persistence of the Product that Defined America* (Basic Books 2007), 451, 462–65.

New People in the New South
An Overview of Southern Immigration

by Carl L. Bankston III

New York, Chicago, and San Francisco are fixed in our imaginations as the great American immigrant settlements. The Immigration Station at Angel Island in the San Francisco Bay, courtesy of the Collections of the Library of Congress.

The classic, stereotypical U.S. immigrant destination is a large city in the North, Midwest, or far West. New York, Chicago, San Francisco are fixed in our imaginations as the great American immigrant settlements. Until recently, most people rarely considered the U.S. South when they thought of new arrivals from other countries. For much of American history the South had very few foreign-born people, and from 1850 to 1970, it was home to a smaller percentage of immigrants than any other region (see Figure 1). Even during the great period of migration from 1880 to 1920, a time when massive waves of newcomers arrived on American shores, only about 2.5 percent of the people in the southern states were foreign-born. After 1970, however, the proportion of southerners who were immigrants began to increase sharply. By 1990 the South had a greater percentage of immigrants than the Midwest, and although the West had become the primary immigrant destination by the end of the twentieth century, its rate of proportional increase had begun to level off somewhat by the early twenty-first century, while the immigrant portion of the South continued to grow. Even the gap between the South and the Northeast, the old immigrant center of the United States, had begun to narrow in the early 2000s.[1]

The primary reason for the South's increase in immigration is economic opportunity, a fundamental motivation for migration. Long existing in pockets of

Figure 1. Percentage of People in the Regions of the United States Who Were Foreigh-Born, 1850–2005

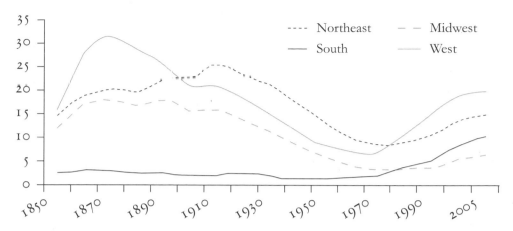

Source: Ruggles et al., 2004.

the South, economic opportunity has become much more widespread and vibrant in recent decades, attracting migrants experiencing worsening conditions in their home countries. In addition, improved means of international transportation enable immigrants to travel greater distances, ranging from more distant home countries to destinations further inside the host countries. Like transportation, improved means of establishing community have increased immigration to the South, and immigrants tend to settle where they establish communities, for reasons of mutual support and access to information about opportunities that often travel along lines of ethnicity or nationality.

The making of a global South is a relatively new phenomenon, yet these dynamics that drive recent immigration to the region have deep historical roots. There is continuity, as well as change, in the integration of the South into a more closely interconnected world. Immigration early in the South's history was a product of the same social and economic forces that have fostered the more recent immigration to the region.

THE OLD SOUTH

In 1850 Louisiana had the largest concentration of immigrants in the South, about 75,000 people and approximately one-quarter of Louisiana's free population. New Orleans, the largest port in the South and the second largest in the nation after New York, was a natural point of entry for people from other countries. Between 1820 and 1860, over half a million immigrants arrived in Louisiana. Given Louisiana's French history and the large French-speaking population in the state during the nineteenth century, it is easy to assume that France would be the place of origin for most of the state's foreign-born residents. Many immigrants to Louisiana were, in fact, from France. About 15,000 people in Louisiana in 1850, or one out of five immigrants in the state, gave France as their birthplace. The largest immigrant group in Louisiana, though, came from Ireland. An estimated 26,580 Louisianans, or nearly 38 percent of the state's immigrants, were born in Ireland in 1850. The Irish are generally described as having arrived in Louisiana in two waves. Those known as the "Old Irish" came primarily from the northern part of Ireland between 1803 and 1830. These earlier immigrants became part of the middle classes of New Orleans. The "New Irish," consisting mainly of peasants, left their homes because of poverty and famine, particularly after the potato blight, which hit Ireland about 1845 and lasted into the following decade, leaving Ireland devastated. They settled in the area known as the City of Lafayette, which was later incorporated into New Orleans and is still identified as the Irish Channel. The New Irish provided much of New Orleans's low-paying manual labor.[2]

Germans made up the second largest immigrant nationality in antebellum Louisiana. Over 20,000 people in the state in 1850, or 28 percent of all immigrants, had been born in Germany. Germans first arrived at the port of New Orleans when Louisiana was a French colony. Many settled just north of New Orleans in the Parishes of St. John and St. Charles, in an area known as the Côte des Allemands, or German Coast. A second wave of peasant German workers followed the first wave of German settlers between 1820 and 1850.[3]

With the Civil War Louisiana ceased to be the immigrant center that it had been in earlier years. By 1900 only about 4 percent of Louisiana's total population and 7 percent of its white population were foreign born. A little over half of these Louisiana immigrants came from Italy and Germany. The Italians's small grocery stores and restaurants left a particularly noticeable mark on New Orleans, as did the high representation of their second and third generations in public service during the twentieth century.[4]

The number of immigrants to Louisiana declined, both in real numbers and as a proportion of the state's population, throughout the period of booming immigration in the industrial North. In 1910 Louisiana had approximately 54,600 foreign-born people, or just over 3 percent of the state's population. Ten years later, this number had dropped by about 4,000 individuals to just under 3 percent of the population. By 1930 fewer than 2 percent of Louisianans were foreign born.[5]

Next to Louisiana, Texas and Maryland were the southern states that had the largest percentage of immigrants before the Civil War. One in ten Texans was foreign born in 1850. Over two-thirds (69 percent) of these Texas immigrants came from Germany. "German Texas" began to take root at the beginning of the 1830s when Johann Friedrich Ernst arrived in New Orleans from Oldenburg in northwestern Germany and learned that land was available in Texas. Ernst obtained a land grant, and his publicity efforts set off a growing migration trend that resulted in a German settlement belt through the southeast area of the state.[6]

Between 1850 and 1900, the German-born population of Texas grew from just under 11,000 to about 49,000. The German-culture population of Texas was much larger; German continued to be a dominant language among many American-born, second- and third-generation German Americans in southeast Texas. During this same period, however, Mexico had become the main source of immigration to the Lone Star State. Mexican immigrants had grown from 22 percent of foreign-born Texans in 1850 to 40 percent in 1900, when Texas became home to about 75,000 Mexicans. Before the beginning of the twentieth century, then, Texas had already begun the shift from European to Mexican immigration that would play a major part in the globalization of the South in the late twentieth century.[7]

The stream of Mexicans to Texas began to flow more rapidly in the early twentieth century as a result of the 1910 Mexican Revolution. At that time about 246,500 people in Texas were foreign-born, or just over 6 percent of the state's population. By 1930 this number had grown to about 437,000, or nearly 8 percent of the population. The number of native-born children of immigrants grew from 6 percent of Texans in 1900 to 8 percent in 1930. Over half of all foreign-born Texans came from Mexico in 1910. This percentage grew to 69 percent by 1920 and to 77 percent by 1930, when Texas was home to over a third of a million people who had been born in Mexico. The number of native-born Texans whose fathers had been born in Mexico grew from 224,000 in 1910 (just under 6 percent of the state's population) to 662,000 in 1930 (about 12 percent). By the end of Mexico's revolutionary years, nearly one out of every five Texans was either of Mexican birth or was the child of a Mexican-born father.

Despite Texas's status as a northern part of Mexico until the Mexican-American War, people of Spanish-speaking origin made up a relatively small percentage of all Texans in 1910: slightly over 3 percent of Texans listed in the U.S. Census had Spanish surnames, and the same percentage gave their "mother tongue" as Spanish. Twenty years later, 10 percent had a Spanish surname and 6 percent identified Spanish as their native language. Largely as a result of this new flow of Mexicans across the border, Texas had the largest number of foreign-born people in the South during the first three decades of the twentieth century.

Maryland, on the border between the South and the North, was home to an estimated 59,500 immigrants in 1850, nearly 12 percent of the state's free population and the largest number of foreign-born people in any southern state except Louisiana. In 1850 Maryland's foreign-born population, like Louisiana's, was primarily the consequence of mid-nineteenth-century immigration from Germany (55 percent) and Ireland (33 percent). These immigrants were heavily concentrated in

The stream of Mexicans to Texas began to flow more rapidly in the early twentieth century as a result The Mexican Revolution. By the end of Mexico's revolutionary years, nearly one out of every five Texans was either of Mexican birth or was the child of a Mexican-born father. Mexican insurrectos with homemade cannon in Juarez, circa 1911, courtesy of the Collections of the Library of Congress.

the port city of Baltimore, where Germans had begun to arrive in the eighteenth century. The potato famine of the 1840s stimulated Irish immigration, while railroad work on the Baltimore-based B&O Railroad supported it. Southwest Baltimore, in particular, became an Irish community during the nineteenth century. The B&O Railroad also opened piers for immigration at Locust Point in 1868, making Baltimore a primary point of entry for immigrants to the United States.[8]

Nineteenth-century immigration to the South, then, was heavily concentrated and tended to arrive through the port cities of New Orleans and Baltimore. Even the Germans who settled in southeast Texas had arrived by way of New Orleans. These pockets of immigration in the South reflected the national origins, chiefly Germany and Ireland, of other nineteenth-century arrivals. Only Texas, with its long border with Mexico, had a large number of people from Latin America.

The pattern of early southern immigration can explain why most southern states were relatively unconnected to global movements until recently, and it can provide a basis for understanding why the South became part of a more globally connected world in the late twentieth and early twenty-first century. As a settled agricultural region, most of the South had few economic opportunities to offer immigrants. The industrial jobs that drew people from around the world to northern cities in the late 1800s and early 1900s were largely absent from the South, where the economy continued to be dominated by small-scale agriculture or by post-Civil War versions of plantation agriculture. New land for farmers was becoming available in the West, not the South, during the 1800s. The one state that did pull in European immigrants, Texas, was the one that overlaps the South and the West, and it attracted German immigrants because of the availability of land. Maryland, a southern boundary state, provided jobs in the railroad industry, creating the infrastructure of the expanding U.S. industrial system.

Immigrants leave homelands, as well as go to host countries, and events shape which original homelands send people to new destinations. The chief southern immigrants from the beginning of the nineteenth to the first half of the twentieth century were Irish, German, and Mexican. The first two nationalities also made up the largest groups of immigrants in other parts of the United States. Lack of economic opportunity in the homeland and a potato famine concentrated in Ireland that extended to Germany helped to stimulate emigration from these countries in the middle of the nineteenth century. The political and social unrest in Mexico, in the early twentieth century, pushed people into the United States.

Finally, ethnic networks and ethnic communities helped to create the early southern pockets of immigrant settlement. Once German settlers had reached southeastern Texas, other Germans were drawn to the same area because of familiarity of language and culture and because information about opportunities often travels along national or ethnic lines of communication.

While immigrant movement into the new South of the late twentieth century may, on the surface, look like a radical break with the demographic patterns of the old, there is a good deal of continuity. The dynamics of immigration—economic opportunity, geographical access, motivations to leave a homeland, and immigrant communities—continued to operate, shifting to encourage migration to new locations. Texas, as one of North America's primary points of entry from Mexico, gave early indications of what would become a dominant trend in late twentieth-century immigration.

IMMIGRATION AREAS OF THE NEW SOUTH

By the end of the twentieth century, the southern states fell roughly into three categories in relation to immigration. Those with the largest foreign populations were the two "access" states, Texas and Florida. These two states, with well over 2.5 million foreign-born residents each in 2000, were points of entry into the United States. Located at the western and eastern edges of the most southern end of the South, these were states of primary migration. Texas simply expanded the role it had played earlier in the century, providing overland access from the south. With the transportation system and widespread economic opportunities of the late twentieth century, though, Texas both drew immigrants from farther south, bringing in increasing numbers of Central Americans, and served as a way station in sending immigrants farther north. Florida, taking over the part played by Louisiana in the nineteenth century, received immigrants by sea.

The "opportunity" states, primarily located in the upper South, made up the second category: Georgia, Maryland, North Carolina, and Virginia. Offering jobs in rapidly rising industries, these four states had immigrant populations of around a half-million each. Access, of course, was important to migration to the economic-opportunity states, and Texas and Florida also provided substantial job opportunities to immigrants.[9]

The final category, the "limited migration" states, are located in the lower or Deep South, with the exception of Arkansas and Tennessee. At least until 2005, these states have continued to have a relatively low immigrant presence by the standards of the late-twentieth-century United States. Even among the limited migration states, though, immigrants have arrived in larger numbers than in earlier years, and new developments, such as the demand for construction workers along the Gulf Coast, could rapidly increase immigration. In Arkansas and Tennessee, the same types of jobs responsible for much higher levels of immigration to Georgia and North Carolina have attracted growing numbers of immigrants, particularly from Mexico and Central America.[10]

TEXAS AND FLORIDA, ACCESS STATES

Texas not only has the greatest number of immigrants in the South, it is third in the nation as an immigrant state of settlement, after California and New York. In the late twentieth century, Mexico, the source of more immigrants to the United States than any other country, saw more of its residents head north as a consequence of economic problems. Over 70 percent of Mexico's export revenues came from oil at the beginning of the 1980s. Beginning in about 1982, a decline in the price of oil provoked a debt crisis, and the country's already existing problems of poverty became worse. Legal Mexican immigration to the United States increased rapidly, from a little over 621,000 in the decade 1970-79 to over 1 million in the 1980s. The 1986 Immigration Reform and Control Act (IRCA) encouraged some unauthorized Mexican immigrants to remain by offering amnesty and encouraged others to move into the United States on a long-term basis by intensifying control of the border, making it more difficult to move back and forth. The extended time frame allowed many workers to seek work further north, away from the border. In 1994 a second economic shock, the devaluation of the peso, caused dramatic inflation and a decline in living standards. In response to the economic problems, over 2.75 million Mexicans legally immigrated to the United States during the 1990s, and from 2000 to 2005 the United States received an average of 200,000 legal permanent residents from Mexico every year.[11]

Undocumented migration showed the same trend, with the largest number of undocumented immigrants arriving from Mexico, motivated both by the economic difficulties at home and by U.S. immigration enforcement activities after IRCA. The number of undocumented immigrants increased by 130,000 each year during the 1970s to an estimated 300,000 annually in the 1980s, and their numbers continued to go up in the following decades. Although many undocumented immigrants arrived by air, often as visitors who stayed after their visas expired, crossing the border from the south was the main method of entering the United States without legal permission. Consequently, these migrants entered the states bordering Mexico. Texas has become the primary access location for Mexicans and South Americans, both those remaining in Texas and those bound for other parts of the U.S. South. By 2005 Texas had an estimated 1,360,000 unauthorized immigrants, or 13 percent of all those in the country, a number second only to California.[12]

The 2000 U.S. Census counted nearly three million immigrants in Texas and three-quarters of these were from Latin America (see Table 1). Just five years later, the American Community Survey of the Census Bureau estimated the state's foreign-born population at over three and a half million. Mexicans made up over 60 percent of all immigrants in Texas in 2000 and 2005. During that same period, an estimated 6 to 7 percent of Texas immigrants were Central Americans. Most of the Central Americans had entered by way of Mexico, again highlighting the role of geographic access.[13]

As a consequence of geographic access, Texas's main immigrant population is Hispanic or Latino, yet Texas also has a substantial Asian minority (see Table 1), attributable to some extent to the general rise in Asian migration around the United States and to the booming economy in Texas cities such as Houston. In 2000 the Vietnamese were Texas's single largest Asian immigrant group, accounting for one out of every four foreign-born Asian Texans, and the state had the second largest Vietnamese population in the United States, after California, with 12 percent of all Vietnamese in the United States.

The case of the Vietnamese illustrates the importance of Texas as a point of access even for members of these more distant national-origin groups. Initial U.S. government resettlement efforts in 1975 had planted Vietnamese communities in the cities of Dallas and Houston. Additional Vietnamese Americans were drawn to Texas by the existing ethnic communities, combined with the availability of jobs in that state. Shrimping became something of an ethnic specialty for Vietnamese Americans along the Gulf Coast of Texas and other states.[14]

In recent times, Florida, the other geographic access state, has been the fourth largest national center of immigration in the United States. The state's immigrant population may actually be much bigger than census statistics indicate; immigration officials believe that about 850,000 undocumented immigrants lived in Florida in 2005, making it the state with the third largest undocumented popula-

Table 1. Regions of Origin of Immigrants in the South and in the U.S., 2000 (Percent in Parentheses)

State	Europe	Asia	Africa	Oceania	Latin America	North America	Total
Alabama	18,415	26,235	3,662	529	35,574	3,352	87,767
	(21.0)	(29.9)	(4.2)	(0.6)	(40.5)	(3.8)	(100.0)
Arkansas	10,028	15,846	1,503	1,165	43,309	1,839	73,690
	(13.6)	(21.5)	(2.0)	(1.6)	(58.8)	(2.5)	(100.0)
Florida	355,427	231,976	34,495	4,957	1,943,781	100,158	2,670,794
	(13.3)	(8.7)	(1.3)	(0.2)	(72.8)	(3.8)	(100.0)
Georgia	74,257	145,696	40,423	2,021	300,357	14,519	577,273
	(12.9)	(25.2)	(7.0)	(0.4)	(52.0)	(2.5)	(100.0)
Louisiana	18,062	43,464	4,016	577	46,561	3,200	115,880
	(15.6)	(37.5)	(3.5)	(0.5)	(40.2)	(2.8)	(100.0)
Maryland	86,840	181,504	62,688	1,957	176,026	9,300	518,315
	(16.8)	(35.0)	(12.1)	(0.4)	(34.0)	(1.8)	(100.0)
Mississippi	7,643	14,434	1,270	249	14,582	1,726	39,904
	(19.2)	(36.2)	(3.2)	(0.6)	(36.5)	(4.3)	(100.0)
North Carolina	60,222	93,133	20,369	1,825	239,853	14,598	430,000
	(14.0)	(21.7)	(4.7)	(0.4)	(55.8)	(3.4)	(100.0)
South Carolina	27,177	29,402	3,248	825	49,608	5,718	115,978
	(23.4)	(25.4)	(2.8)	(0.7)	(42.8)	(4.9)	(100.0)
Tennessee	28,117	50,584	8,696	929	63,484	7,194	159,004
	(17.7)	(31.8)	(5.5)	(0.6)	(39.9)	(4.5)	(100.0)
Texas	152,327	466,218	64,470	6,984	2,172,476	37,165	2,899,640
	(5.3)	(16.1)	(2.2)	(0.2)	(74.9)	(1.3)	(100.0)
Virginia	86,612	235,374	42,509	2,807	189,809	13,160	570,271
	(15.2)	(41.3)	(7.5)	(0.5)	(33.3)	(2.3)	(100.0)
U.S.	4,772,270	8,364,026	839,547	180,308	15,471,784	836,068	31,107,573
	(15.7)	(26.4)	(2.8)	(0.6)	(50.8)	(2.7)	(100.0)

Source: U.S. Census Bureau, Census 2000, Summary Tape File 3, Selected Social Characteristics (DP-2).

tion. As in Texas, Hispanics constitute about two-thirds of the immigrants. In the case of Florida, though, geographic access came by sea and air from the south. In 2000 about one-fourth of Florida immigrants had been born in Cuba, and 16 to 17 percent were from the rest of the Caribbean region. South Americans made up an additional 15 percent, with Central Americans and Mexicans trailing at 9 and 7 percents, respectively.[15]

In Louisiana and Maryland the early foreign-born population was primarily the consequence of mid-nineteenth-century immigration from Germany and Ireland. Harper's Weekly *illustration of German immigrants embarking for the New World, courtesy of the Collections of the Library of Congress.*

Like the Irish and Mexican migrations, the Cuban influx had been stimulated by problems at home. The first wave came between 1959 and 1962, when about 215,000 middle- and upper-class Cubans began pouring into the United States in the early years of Fidel Castro's revolutionary government. Following the 1962 Cuban Missile Crisis, travel between the two countries became much more difficult; until 1965 only about 30,000 Cubans managed to leave the island for the United States. In the autumn of 1965, though, Castro invited his critics to leave the country, and President Lyndon B. Johnson responded by inviting them to find freedom in the United States. In this second wave, which lasted until 1973, 340,000 Cubans made their way to the United States. A final wave of Cuban refugees left the island in 1980 in the Mariel boatlifts, which brought more than 125,000 refugees from Cuba to the United States over a six-month period.[16]

Although Cuban migration had been limited since the Mariel era, Cubans are at present the largest single ethnic group in the state. In 2000 there were 846,080 Cubans in Florida, and by 2005 the number of Floridians identified as Cuban had reached over one million, or one out of every seventeen people in the state. In Miami, one-third of the residents were Cuban in the early twenty-first century.[17]

The Spanish-speaking environment of southern Florida helped to create communities that attracted and often held people from the Caribbean and South

America. In 2000, 31 percent of all Colombians, the largest group of South American immigrants in the United States, were concentrated in Florida. Many of the South Americans, especially the numerous Colombians, were motivated to migrate by social unrest and violence in their homelands. The booming economy of Florida, in part created by Cuban ethnic enterprise, both attracted immigrants and encouraged them to remain.[18]

OPPORTUNITY STATES

In 1970 Georgia, at the forefront of the economic opportunity states, was home to 32,988 immigrants, who made up less than 1 percent of the state's population. Ten years later, this number had increased to 91,480, or slightly fewer than 2 percent of the population, and by 1990 to 173,126 immigrants, or nearly 3 percent of the population. By 2000 this number increased more than three-fold during the 1990s, reaching 577,273, or 7 percent of the state's population (see Table 1). This remarkable growth continued into the new century, reaching an estimated 795,000, or 9 percent of the population, by 2005. By that year, Georgia was seventh in the nation in undocumented immigrants, with an estimated 470,000 foreign-born individuals without proper papers living in the state.[19]

The majority of the new population has been Hispanic, with Mexicans making up the largest part of Georgia's recent immigration boom. In the early 2000s, about one-third of all the state's foreign-born people came from Mexico. Central Americans placed a distant second, accounting for 6 to 7 percent, followed by the Caribbean, with 5 to 6 percent.[20]

This rapid growth in Mexican immigrant laborers can be traced to an increase in the supply of workers from the south and in the demand for workers in Georgia's industry. As Mexico's economic problems in the 1980s and 1990s encouraged more people to look for work north of the border, the newcomers began to look further than the border states. By 2000 the most common industrial concentrations of Mexicans in Georgia were construction (34 percent of Mexican workers), agriculture (8 percent), carpets and rugs (6 percent), and meat products (5 percent). The last two were new industries in Georgia that had acquired dominant positions in the national and world economy.[21]

In the 1970s and 1980s, the American meat-processing industry became more consolidated and began moving out of urban to more rural areas. Skill requirements fell in these highly mechanized, large-scale meat-processing plants, and the industry began to hire more immigrants, with the proportion of immigrants rising from 8 percent of workers in 1980 to 35 percent in 2000. During the 1970s, Gainesville, in north Georgia, became known as "the Poultry Capital of the World," processing chicken meat for shipping to national and global markets. The first Mexican workers began arriving in northern Georgia in the 1970s, establishing a basis for network support and communication for future arrivals. Their numbers began to take off during the 1980s, as more Mexican workers moved north looking for work and work became increasingly available in processing. By the 1990s the Spanish-speaking population of the small town of Gainesville, with an official total population in 1990 of 17,885, may have numbered as many as 30,000.[22]

During the 1950s and 1960s, northeast textile and carpet manufacturing businesses, which had begun to relocate to the South as early as the 1920s, drawn by the competitive advantages of the South's lower wages, established a rapidly increasing presence in northwest Georgia. This area, particularly the town of Dalton, emerged as a center of this industry, producing 80 percent of all the carpet in the United States by the late 1990s. Mexican workers who had come to work in north Georgia's poultry industry in the mid-1980s found other regional opportunities, including the carpet industry. Other Mexican immigrants, pushed further north by a slowdown in the Texas building industry, as well as by the longer-term orientation created by American immigration policy, came to the area. Perceptions of a labor shortage among carpet manufacturing employers in this small town combined with the relatively low wages that new Mexican immigrants would accept made the new arrivals attractive to employers, and Mexicans moved into the industry on a large scale during the 1990s. From 1990 to 2000, the Hispanic portion of Dalton's population grew from under 7 to over 40 percent.[23]

Along with the development of new industries, agriculture, particularly in the form of large-scale agribusiness, continues to be an important economic activity in Georgia, particularly in the south. Ninety percent of the state's symbolic peaches are produced by five growers in Fruit County. In addition, bell peppers, lima beans, pole beans, southern peas, sweet corn, and tomatoes are important crops. During the 1980s, growers increasingly began to draw on Mexican labor for the low-paying but necessary work of planting and harvesting. By 2000 about one out of every twelve Mexicans in the Georgia labor force was in agriculture.[24]

Although Georgia's new industries and agriculture provided jobs that attracted immigrants moving up from the border states, the dynamo of Atlanta was the greatest source of economic opportunity for the state's immigrants, including the Hispanic population. In 1990 metropolitan Atlanta had a total population of 2,833,511 and an immigrant population of 115,642. Ten years later, greater Atlanta's population had grown to 4,112,198 and its immigrants had increased to 423,105, or nearly three quarters of all the immigrants in the state. Of these new arrivals, 170,510 had entered the United States between 1995 and 2000. Seventy percent of the state's foreign-born Asians and 57 percent of its Hispanic population lived in metropolitan Georgia in 2000. While men and women made up roughly equal portions of Asian immigrants, men outnumbered women by more than ten to one among Hispanics immigrants. The Hispanic newcomers who had

U.S. government resettlement efforts in 1975 planted Vietnamese communities in the cities of Dallas and Houston. Soon, existing ethnic communities and the availability of jobs in Texas inspired other Vietnamese immigrants to make their way to the state, and by 2000 the Vietnamese were the single largest Asian immigrant group. South Vietnamese refugees walking across a U.S. Navy vessel, courtesy of Wikimedia Commons.

come north, mainly from Texas, were mostly men either single or traveling without their families, who were attracted to the availability of blue-collar jobs created by the Atlanta economy. Nearly 40 percent of Atlanta's Mexicans were in construction (up from 33 percent in the state in general), providing the labor to build the rapidly growing city. Another 12 percent were in manufacturing.[25]

As a world center, Atlanta has attracted a diverse Asian population. The largest grouping of Atlanta's Asians in 2000 consisted of people from the South Asian subcontinent, with just under 36,000 Asian Indians, over 1,000 Bangladeshis, and well over 3,000 Pakistanis. At that time, Atlanta was also home to nearly 25,000 Vietnamese, close to 22,000 Koreans, and just under 21,500 Chinese. Largely members of an educated work force, the South Asian migrants were drawn to this international-airport-hub city by its professional, white-collar opportunities in professional, scientific, and technical industries, which in 2000 employed one in five of the Asian Indians in the metropolis.

As in Texas, the Vietnamese first came to Atlanta as part of government resettlement efforts, and the initial Vietnamese communities provided bases for secondary migration from other parts of the country while Vietnamese job seekers looked for work. They found it in the blue-collar sector, with nearly one-third of Atlanta Vietnamese occupied in the city's manufacturing industry in 2000. Koreans, as in New York and Los Angeles, became the small shopkeepers of Greater Atlanta, with about 22 percent of Koreans in retail trade. Chinese, like the South Asians, had often come with educational credentials to seek jobs in professional, scientific, and technical fields, which held 17 percent of the area's Chinese workers. Other Chinese migrants tended to go in to restaurant and related work, as accommodations and food services held 16 percent of the city's Chinese workers. A diversified metropolitan economy with global connections had pulled in workers from all over the world into a mosaic of national-origin specializations.

North Carolina shares many of the characteristics of Georgia, without having an urban center to parallel Atlanta. In 2000 Mexicans made up 75 percent of North Carolina's Hispanic immigrants, and Central Americans, who had presumably almost all entered the United States through Mexico, made up another 15 percent. By 2005 North Carolina was ninth in the nation in undocumented immigrants, with an estimated 350,000, which means that the actual number of Hispanics in the state may have been much greater than indicated by census statistics. As in Georgia, the most common industrial concentration for Hispanic workers in 2000 was construction, which employed 26 percent of them. Another 11 percent were employed in agriculture.[26]

By 2005 North Carolina employed a greater proportion of Hispanic immigrants in agriculture than did Georgia because of the large number of construction jobs in the booming region of Atlanta. However, North Carolina did have its own rapidly growing Sunbelt-economy cities, providing employment for new arrivals. In North Carolina, as in Georgia, Hispanic construction workers tended to be found in the larger cities, particularly in Charlotte (which, with over 40,000 Hispanics, had the largest number in the state), Raleigh, Winston-Salem, Durham, and Greensboro.[27]

Farming is important in North Carolina, placing it eighth in the nation in total agricultural income. In the past, African Americans did most of the state's low-paid, seasonal work demanded by agriculture, but the increasing availability of workers moving northward from Mexico made them an appealing source of labor. By the 1990s North Carolina, which was fifth in the United States in numbers of migrant workers, drew nine out of ten of its farm workers from the ranks of the Hispanics.[28]

North Carolina is not normally thought of as a center of the American South Asian population. Nevertheless, over 25,000 Asian Indians lived in the state in 2000, about 20,000 of whom were foreign-born. The North Carolina Asian Indians tended to be an urban population: 40 percent were located in the cities of Charlotte, Raleigh, Durham, or Greensboro, and one out of every four Asian Indians in North Carolina lived in the metropolitan area of Charlotte-Gastonia-Rock Hill. These largely urban immigrants were, as elsewhere in the South, concentrated in professional fields: 18 percent of employed Asian Indians in North Carolina were in professional, technical, and scientific industries, and another 19 percent were in educational, health, and social services fields.[29]

The 18,500 Chinese and 12,400 Koreans in North Carolina were also part of the urban landscape, with one out of five of the former and one out of four of the latter living in the Charlotte-Gastonia-Rock Hill metropolis in 2000. The Chinese were most heavily concentrated in professional fields and food services, while Koreans tended to be in retail trade or professional, scientific, and technical areas. The wake of the Vietnam War had brought a fairly large Southeast Asian population to North Carolina, with 15,600 Vietnamese, 7,000 Hmong, 5,000 Lao, and 2,300 Cambodians living in the state in 2000.[30]

Virginia and Maryland shared in a cluster of service and professional industries heavily concentrated in the highly populated area around the District of Columbia. Virginia was close to Georgia in total numbers of immigrants in 2000, but had a much higher proportion of Asian immigrants (see Table 1). Virginia's Fairfax County, part of the D.C. area, held 42 percent of the state's immigrants in 2000 and immigrants made up one fourth of the county population. The two D.C.-area counties of Prince George's and Montgomery contained two-thirds of Maryland's immigrant population, and immigrants made up 14 percent of the people in Prince George's and over one-fourth of the people in Montgomery.[31]

The service and professional industry character of many of the job opportunities in these two states helps to explain why there were more Asian immigrants in each, proportionately and in numbers, than there were in Georgia. Virginia's largest Asian group, Asian Indians (47,500 in 2000), were represented most heavily in professional, scientific, and technical fields, which employed one-fourth of them, followed by retail trade, educational health and social services, and accommodations and food services (largely the hotel/motel industry). Chinese people in Virginia, the second largest Asian group (35,500 in 2000), tended to be most concentrated in accommodations and food services, and then in professional,

The first wave of large-scale Cuban migration to Florida occurred when middle and upper-class Cubans began pouring into the United States in the early years of Fidel Castro's revolutionary government. Following the Cuban Missile Crisis of 1962, travel between Cuba and the United States became much more difficult. President John F. Kennedy and advisors on the West Wing Colonnade after the crisis's EXCOMM Meeting on October 29, 1962. Left to right: Special Assistant McGeorge Bundy, President Kennedy, Assistant Secretary of Defense Paul Nitze, Chairman of the Joint Chiefs of Staff General Maxwell Taylor, Secretary of Defense Robert McNamara. Photograph by White House photographer Cecil Stoughton, courtesy of Wikimedia Commons.

scientific, and technical fields. Maryland looked similar to Virginia in numbers of Asian Indians (49,800) and Chinese (49,500) and in industrial concentrations.[32]

Southeast Asians, especially Vietnamese, tended to be located more in Virginia than in Maryland in 2000. The former was home to 35,400 Vietnamese and the latter to 16,700. Again, the Southeast Asians had originally settled in the area as a result of the U.S. Government refugee program and had remained because of the existence of ethnic communities and job opportunities. The Vietnamese in this region were employed most often in manufacturing or retail trade, but by 2000 many were also in the area's plentiful professional, technical, and scientific occupations.

As elsewhere, Hispanics were most often in construction, which employed 17 percent of them in Virginia and 18 percent in Maryland. This was particularly true for the largest Hispanic group, Mexicans. In both states, one in five Mexicans was in construction.

LIMITED MIGRATION STATES

The states of the Deep South, Arkansas, and Tennessee still tended to attract fewer immigrants than the rest of the country at the turn of the last century. James R. Elliott and Marcel Ionescu, sociologists at Tulane University, attributed the limited migration to the "Deep South triad" of Louisiana, Mississippi, and Alabama to their relatively stagnant economies, pointing out that they contained some of the slowest growing metropolitan areas in the country. All of the limited migration states also showed low median household incomes. Mississippi, with the least immigration among the southern states, also had the lowest household median income in the 2000 U.S. Census, at $31,330.[33]

Louisiana had largely lost its centrality as a place of entry into the United States by the twentieth century, with the port of New Orleans steadily losing ground to other ports and to forms of transportation and communication other than the sea. By the late twentieth century, then, the Deep South had not been pulled as deeply into the global movement of people because it offered neither access nor opportunity on the same scale as the other southern states. However, although slower to develop international connections than other areas, Arkansas and the lower South did participate in the overall increase in immigration that affected the rest of the country.

The Asian population, especially the Southeast Asian population, was an early immigrant group in these states. Louisiana, in particular, had a fairly large Asian population, with over 43,000 individuals in 2000. The Vietnamese were particularly concentrated along the Gulf Coast region of Louisiana and Mississippi because of the relative abundance of economic opportunities afforded by cities such as New Orleans and Biloxi. In both states, about one out of every ten Vietnamese men in 2000 was employed in agriculture and fishing, primarily in shrimping and fishing in the Gulf of Mexico.[34]

South Carolina, with the largest recorded Hispanic population among the limited migration states in 2000, employed one out of five Hispanic workers in construction and another one out of five in manufacturing. The industrial concentration of Hispanics, then, is similar to that found in other areas of the South, and the movement of Latino immigrant workers to South Carolina can be expected to increase as jobs in construction and manufacturing increase.[35]

Louisiana had a reported Hispanic immigrant population of 46,561 in 2000 (see Table 1). The number of Hispanic immigrants entering the state from Texas increased during the 1990s in response to a demand for labor in oil-related construction, particularly in shipbuilding and ship repair, in the southwestern part of the state, with companies in the areas of Morgan City and Houma-Thibodeaux recruiting the abundant skilled and semi-skilled construction labor available in south Texas.[36]

In 1990s Mississippi and Alabama, Hispanic workers moved into the Gulf Coast area to work in jobs in casino construction and forestry. Although small in absolute size and relative ranking, the foreign-born populations in Alabama and Mississippi approximately doubled and experienced a higher rate of growth than did the nation as a whole during the 1990s. Louisiana, on the other hand, experienced a slower pace of growth (32.6 percent increase), leading to a substantial drop in its foreign-born state ranking, from twenty-sixth in 1990 to nineteenth in 2000.[37]

The big boom in Hispanic migration to the Central Gulf Coast followed Hurricane Katrina in the Fall of 2005, with an estimated 100,000 Hispanic workers moving into the region. In the days after the hurricane, President George W. Bush temporarily suspended the Davis-Bacon Act, which guarantees construction workers the prevailing local wage when paid with federal money. The Hispanic population of New Orleans is believed to have increased by 4,000 people as a result of the influx of disaster restoration workers; that of neighboring Jefferson Parish had increased by 6,000, so that by early 2007 one out of ten people in both New Orleans and Jefferson Parish were Hispanic. Many had come straight from Texas, but others had entered the country earlier through Texas or another border access state and then migrated to the Gulf Coast.[38]

In short, the hurricane had created a demand for exactly the type of work that was already an ethnic specialization for Mexican and Central American job seekers: construction. The southern-most part of the Deep South triad became a new setting for economic demand that was bringing it more closely into the global system of labor exchange.

Arkansas and Tennessee had seen rapid growth in their Hispanic populations over the course of the 1990s. Arkansas's total Hispanic population, native and

Louisiana, with the largest port in the South and the second largest in the nation, was a major center of immigration in the nineteenth century. The state already had lost its distinction as a place of entry into the country by the twentieth century, when World War II Federal Art Project posters were warning of the need for port security. Courtesy of the Collections of the Library of Congress.

foreign born, had grown from 19,586 in 1990 to 43,309 in 2000, with Mexicans constituting over 70 percent of the state's Hispanics. The native-born and immigrant Hispanic population of Tennessee had grown from 31,075 to 63,484 during that same period, according to U.S. Census estimates. This remarkable increase (see Table 1) was due to jobs available in the poultry industry and to construction jobs.

During the twentieth century the United States as a whole became more closely integrated in global interconnections, and the southern part of the nation became a more vibrant part of the American economy. These two historical developments have stimulated the driving forces of economic opportunity, transportation, communication, and concentrations of settlement in the South. Most of the increase in immigration to the South, as well as to other parts of the country, has been due to the rapid growth of Asian and Hispanic newcomers. Asians have come to the United States because of the growing links between the United States and Asia. American military intervention in Southeast Asia, and the refugee movements that followed that intervention, played a large part in creating Asian communities throughout the United States. As we have seen, this was the source of several of the largest Asian communities in southern states, particularly in the states along the Gulf Coast. However, even those settlements that had their origins in government-sponsored refugee programs continued and grew because of the existence of economic opportunity.

In the South, as well as in the United States as a whole, Hispanics constituted the largest numbers of immigrants. In part, this has been due to access, and the largest Hispanic centers in the South have emerged in Texas and Florida because of the geographic location of these states. Again, however, opportunity has been a key issue, since immigrants seek access because of relative disadvantages in their original homelands and relative advantages in their destinations. Moreover, these access states would not have retained immigrants if jobs had not been available.

Movement into the access states has been part of a chain of historical events. For Texas, these events go back to the early part of the century, so that the new migration should be seen as the latest manifestation of historic links between events south of the border and movement across the border. For Florida, most of the historic events are more recent, although there is a long-standing connection between Florida and the nations of the Caribbean. Throughout the South, growing industries have pulled in immigrants, primarily into the opportunity states, but also into states that are slower in entering the global labor market.

NOTES

1. Carl L. Bankston III, "Immigrants in the New South: An Introduction," *Sociological Spectrum* 23 (April 2003): 123–28; Carol Schmid, "Immigration and Asian and Hispanic Minorities in the New South: An Exploration of History, Attitudes, and Demographic Trends," *Sociological Spectrum* 23 (April 2003): 129–58.

2. Steven Ruggles, Matthew Sobek, Trent Alexander, Catherine A. Fitch, Ronald Goeken, Patricia Kelly Hall, Miriam King, and Chad Ronnander, *Integrated Public Use Microdata Series: Version 3.0* [Machine-readable database], Minnesota Population Center [producer and distributor], 2004, http://www.ipums.org; (Decennial Ipums Files 1850–2000) (Minnesota Population Center [producer and distributor], 2004); U.S. Census Bureau, *American Community Survey File, 2005* (U.S. Census Bureau [producer and distributor], 2006). John Finn, *New Orleans Irish: Famine Exiles* (Holy Family Church, 1977), 1–17.

3. John H. Deiler, *The Settlement of the German Coast of Louisiana and the Creoles of German Descent* (Philadelphia, Germanica Press), 45–60.

4. Anthony V. Margavio and Jerome J. Salamone, *Bread and Respect: The Italians of Louisiana* (Pelican Publishing, 2002), 34–42.

5. Statistics in this paragraph are drawn from Ruggles et al., *Integrated Public Use Microdata Series.*

6. Rudolf L. Biesele, *The History of the German Settlements in Texas, 1831–1861* (German-Texan Heritage Society), 1–25.

7. The data on Mexican immigration to Texas are derived from Ruggles et al., *Integrated Public Use Microdata Series.*

8. M. Mark Stolarik, *Forgotten Doors: The Other Ports of Entry to the United States* (Balch Institute Press, 1988), 44–66.

9. U.S. Census Bureau, *Census 2000, Summary Tape File 3*, Selected Social Characteristics (DP-2).

10. U.S. Census Bureau, *American Community Survey File, 2005*.

11. United States Department of Homeland Security, *Yearbook of Immigration Statistics, 2005* (U.S. Department of Homeland Security, Office of Immigration Statistics, 2006), 6–11.

12. Michael Hoefer, Nancy Rytina, and Christopher Campbell, *Estimates of the Unauthorized Immigrant Population Residing in the United States: January, 2005* (Department of Homeland Security, Office of Immigration Statistics, 2006), 1–2.

13. See Table 1 for statistics on 2000. Estimates for 2005 are drawn from U.S. Census Bureau, *American Community Survey File, 2005*.

14. Rubén G. Rumbaut, "Vietnam," in *The New Americans: A Guide to Immigration since 1965*, ed. Mary C. Waters and Reed Ueda with Helen B. Marrow (Harvard University Press, 2007), 652–73.

15. Data on undocumented immigrants are from Michael Hoefer et al., *Estimates of the Unauthorized Immigrant Population*, 8; data on immigrants in general are from Ruggles et al., *Integrated Public Use Microdata Series*, and U.S. Census Bureau, *American Community Survey File, 2005*.

16. Lisandro Perez, "Cuba," in *The New Americans: A Guide to Immigration since 1965*, 386–98.

17. The estimate of one-third of the Miami population comes from Alex Stepick, Guillermo Grenier, Max Castro, and Marvin Dunn. *This Land Is Our Land: Immigrants and Power in Miami* (University of California Press, 2003), 35.

18. For information on the Colombian population, see Helen B. Marrow, "South America," in *The New Americans: A Guide to Immigration since 1965*, 593–611.

19. Hoefer et al., *Estimates of the Unauthorized Immigrant Population*, 8.

20. U.S. Census Bureau, *Census 2000, Summary Tape File 4, Total Population (by Detailed Race)* (PCT-1).

21. U.S. Census Bureau, *Census 2000, Summary Tape File 4, Industry (by Detailed Race)* (PCT-85).

22. For background and statistics on immigrants in the Georgia poultry industry, I draw chiefly from Neeraj Kaushal, Cordelia W. Reimers, and David M. Reimers, "Immigrants and the Economy," in *The New Americans: A Guide to Immigration since 1965*, 176–88; and Greig Guthey, "Mexican Places in Southern Spaces: Globalization, Work, and Daily Life in and around the North Georgia Poultry Industry," in *Latino Workers in the Contemporary South*, ed. Arthur D. Murphy, Colleen Blanchard, and Jennifer A. Hill (University of Georgia Press, 2001), 57–67. Guthey, "Mexican Places in Southern Spaces," 58.

23. My information on the Dalton carpet industry and its immigrant population comes from conversations with the foremost scholar on this topic, Rubén Hernández-León, as well as from the following authoritative published work authored with Victor Zúñiga: "Making Carpet by the Mile: The Emergence of a Mexican Immigrant Community in an Industrial Region of the U.S. Historic South," *Social Science Quarterly* 81 (March 2000):49–66; "Mexican Immigrant Communities in the South and Social Capital: The Case of Dalton, Georgia," *Southern Rural Sociology* 19.1 (2003): 20–45; "Appalachia Meets Aztlán: Mexican Immigration and Intergroup Relations in Dalton, Georgia" in *New Destinations: Mexican Immigration in the United States*, ed. Victor Zúñiga and Rubén Hernández-León (Russell Sage Foundation), 244–75. Statistics from Hernández-León and Zúñiga, "Appalachia Meets Aztlán," 247.

24. U.S. Census Bureau, *Census 2000, Summary Tape File 4, Industry (by Detailed Race)* (PCT-85).

25. The statistics on immigration to Atlanta are drawn from U.S. Census Bureau, *Census 2000, Summary Tape File 4, Total Population (by Detailed Race)* (PCT-1); U.S. Census Bureau, *Census 2000, Summary Tape File 4, Industry (by Detailed Race)* (PCT-85).

26. Data on undocumented immigrants in North Carolina from Hoefer et al., *Estimates of the Unauthorized Immigrant Population*, 8.

27. U.S. Census Bureau, *American Community Survey File, 2005*; U.S. Census Bureau, *Census 2000, Summary Tape File 4, Industry (by Detailed Race)* (PCT-85).

28. The rankings of North Carolina in agricultural income and numbers of immigrant workers come from Jack G. Dale, Susan Andreatta, and Elizabeth Freeman, "Language and the Migrant Worker Experience in Rural North Carolina," in *Latino Workers in the Contemporary South*, ed. Arthur D. Murphy, Colleen Blanchard, and Jennifer A. Hill (University of Georgia Press, 2001), 96–97.

29. U.S. Census Bureau, *Census 2000, Summary Tape File 4, Industry (by Detailed Race)* (PCT-85).

30. Ibid.; U.S. Census Bureau, *Census 2000, Summary Tape File 4, Total Population (by Detailed Race)* (PCT-1).

31. U.S. Census Bureau, *Census 2000, Summary Tape File 4, Total Population (by Detailed Race)* (PCT-1).

32. Statistics on Asian and Hispanic immigrants in Virginia are drawn from the U.S. Census Bureau, *Census 2000, Summary Tape File 4, Industry (by Detailed Race)* (PCT-85).

33. James R. Elliott and Marcel Ionescu, "Postwar Immigration to the Deep South Triad: What Can a Peripheral Region Tell Us about Immigrant Settlement and Employment?" *Sociological Spectrum* 23 (April 2003): 159–80.

34. U.S. Census, *Census 2000, Summary Tape File 3, Selected Social Characteristics* (DP-2).

35. U.S. Census Bureau, *Census 2000, Summary Tape File 4, Industry (by Detailed Race)* (PCT-85).

36. See Katherine M. Donato, Melissa Stainback, and Carl L. Bankston III, "The Economic Incorporation of Mexican Immigrants in Southern Louisiana: A Tale of Two Cities," in *New Destinations of Mexican Immigration in the United States: Community Formation, Local Responses, and Inter-Group Relations*, 77–78.

37. Donato et al., "The Economic Incorporation of Mexican Immigrants," 77.

38. Estimates are from Mark Waller, "Baby Boom," *The Times-Picayune*, 29 January 2007, A1+.

Your Dekalb Farmers Market
Food and Ethnicity in Atlanta

by Tore C. Olsson

*I*n the summer of 1977, Robert Blazer opened a local farmers market in Decatur, Georgia, only a few miles from the heart of downtown Atlanta. The market began humbly in a former greenhouse with no refrigeration, and Blazer's operation initially served as a simple exchange point between local farmers and consumers. Born into a middle-class family of Italian descent, Blazer grew up in his father's variety store in Pawtucket, Rhode Island, and was quite familiar with the retail food industry. After securing a loan from his family, he moved south with plans to enter the grocery trade himself. His initial goal seemed simple: "to provide the people in the neighborhood with high quality product" and perhaps turn a bit of a profit along the way. In the city of Atlanta, Blazer saw a "traditional" community that reminded him of his New England roots, "especially when it came to cooking."[1]

While the culinary atmosphere of 1977 Atlanta may have remained "traditional," the city itself was hardly reminiscent of the romantic world Margaret Mitchell depicted in her 1939 Civil War epic, *Gone with the Wind*. Having endured the racial turmoil of the Civil Rights Movement without the overt violent conflict that haunted some of its southern neighbors, the Atlanta of the 1970s was a city obsessed with economic progress, and it would undergo tremendous expansion in the last decades of the twentieth century. Just as *Atlanta Constitution* editor Henry Grady had looked north for investment and support in the wake of the Civil War, the city's newest generation of boosters saw international dollars as the future for Atlanta and relentlessly promoted the city's hospitality, cheap labor force, and agreeable business climate.

But despite Atlanta's claims of being an "international city," most of its residents in the 1970s still affirmed stereotypical myths about the homogeneity of a southern biracial society. Atlanta, like the rest of Georgia and the Southeast, had not experienced the massive influx of immigration that transformed northern cities in the early twentieth century, and few tightly knit ethnic communities were noticeable within the city. Although some immigrant groups, notably Jews, Greeks, and, in the 1950s, Cuban refugees, had settled in Atlanta, their numbers were comparatively small, and many of these immigrants arrived with cultural

In the summer of 1977 Robert Blazer opened a local farmers market in Decatur, Georgia, only a few miles from the heart of downtown Atlanta. The market began humbly in a former greenhouse without refrigeration, and Blazer's operation initially served as a simple exchange point between local farmers and consumers. All photographs courtesy of Kelli Guinn.

and financial capital that eased their assimilation into an established society. In a state with nearly five and a half million residents, Georgia was home in 1980 to less than one hundred thousand foreign-born individuals. Less than 1 percent of Georgians classified themselves as outside of the binary racial structure of black and white; in metro Atlanta this number was barely higher. In a matter of two decades, this homogeneity would be considerably upset.[2]

Over the course of nearly thirty years, the "Your Dekalb Farmers Market," like the city itself, was wholly transformed by an immigration revolution that continues to redefine the dynamics of the urban South. What began as a roadside produce stand was a decade later one of the largest indoor food markets in the nation, occupying a facility of over 140,000 square feet and catering to a demographic group that had only recently settled in the region. In today's Dekalb Farmers Market, laden shopping carts collide in crowded aisles, hundreds of voices speaking dozens of languages blend into a jarring cacophony inside the refrigerated warehouse, and nearly two hundred flags from all corners of the globe hang from the rafters, perfectly reflecting the diversity of both the employees and the clientele.

Although the phrase "farmers market" brings to mind images of local growers peddling their produce, Blazer's operation is fully centralized, with all workers officially employed by the market. Out of these nearly five hundred and fifty employees, no more than two dozen are native southerners, black or white, and Blazer claims that his workforce hails from "every area that has a large immigration going on." The Dekalb Market's clientele is similarly diverse. The product line has also shifted to meet the preferences and tastes of its new customers, with bok choy, carp, and samosas for sale alongside okra and collard greens. The Dekalb Farmers Market has thus become an animated monument to a multicultural Atlanta.[3]

While statistical figures can offer only a slice of reality, a comparative analysis of the 1980 and 2000 censuses is solid proof that Atlanta has undergone tremendous change. DeKalb County attracted thousands of immigrants during these two decades, due to the availability of cheap housing and access to public transportation. While the county grew 38 percent in total population between 1980 and 2000, the number of non-white and non-black residents grew by 747 percent, from 1.5 to nearly 10 percent of the population. Comprised mainly of Asian and Latino immigrants and refugees, this wave of newcomers found homes in all of Atlanta's fast-growing communities. In some of the city's suburbs, this increase was especially noticeable. Chamblee, located in northern DeKalb County, was more than 92 percent white in 1980, but twenty years later this number had fallen to 46 percent. Chamblee's foreign-born population simultaneously increased from 6 to 64 percent of the total, eventually earning the suburb the derisive nickname of "Chambodia," although today Latinos are by far the area's largest immigrant group.[4]

This demographic upheaval raises several important questions. How has the introduction of a large immigrant population reshaped southern culture, long known for resisting outside influence? How does cultural and culinary diversity shape regional, ethnic, and racial self-awareness? And in looking at trends within the food industry and Atlanta cuisine, why did the Rebel Chef Drive-In, as an allegorical example, close, while the Thai Diner opened a second location? As demonstrated in the history of the Dekalb Farmers Market, ethnic food, its sale and consumption, was critical to both the dissolution and preservation of identities for both recent immigrants and native southerners; and while the growth of the market was occasionally resisted by natives, it was more often embraced and promoted by those who saw ethnic and cultural diversity as vital to the making of a truly international and cosmopolitan city.

In the course of a quarter century, this tremendous immigrant influx internationalized Atlanta from the bottom-up and deeply affected the way white and black southerners eat, drink, and think about food and themselves. Atlanta's cultural transformation manifested in the rise of the Dekalb Farmers Market and has given a new spin to the adage "You are what you eat."

MAKING A GLOBAL MARKET

The explosion of immigration in the Sunbelt South is a rather new phenomenon, and our understanding of its significance is only now developing. Both journalists and historians are coming to grips with the social, political, economic, and cultural effects of recent immigrants and are finding the worn debate of the "melting pot" versus "multiculturalism" insufficient for fully explaining present issues. Recent publications acknowledge the downfall of the South's binary racial order and discuss the complications that this has brought. As historians and anthropologists recognize the tremendous cultural importance of food and its place within modern consumer societies, we gain an important tool in analyzing the effects of global migrations. Still, much of today's southern food writing is cast in a framework of black and white, despite the addition of Latino, Asian, and African cuisines to the southern diet.

When Robert Blazer opened Your Dekalb Farmers Market in the summer of 1977, however, non-Euro-American foods were fringe delicacies enjoyed only by a small percentage of Atlanta's population. Glancing through the 1977 Atlanta Yellow Pages reveals a city that had yet to be transformed by the proliferation of ethnic food: only ninety-two out of approximately fifteen hundred restaurants could be classified as non-Euro-American. With forty-six Chinese, fourteen Japanese, eighteen Mexican, and only two Thai restaurants, Atlanta was a city still characterized by "all-American" food such as that served at the Varsity and Chick-fil-A, two popular restaurants who both claim Atlanta as their birthplace. Blazer was therefore not incorrect in describing Atlanta's culinary atmosphere as "traditional" upon his arrival.[5]

The very same year that Blazer relocated to Georgia, Herbert T. Jenkins, the former long-time police chief of Atlanta, published a short book on the history of Atlanta's produce business. Titled *Food, Fairs and Farmers' Markets in Atlanta*, Jenkins's book portrayed a city whose food industry truly was as "traditional" as Blazer remembered. In describing the Atlanta State Farmers Market, which was then the largest such venue in the city, Jenkins writes of a "pleasant nostalgic scene" where Georgia farmers brought their harvest directly to local consumers. One annual celebration was the "popular and enduring" Watermelon Day, where free slices of watermelon and live country music were a "big highlight for the entire family." Though "esoteric produce" like "clementines, romaine, [and] shallots" were sold, they did "not comprise a typical Atlanta menu."[6]

It was in this city of grits and greens that Your Dekalb Farmers Market opened on June 2, 1977, at Scott Boulevard and North Decatur Road in Decatur. The local community newspaper described the market as a "new business that will specialize in the sale of fresh fruits and vegetables." The *Decatur-DeKalb News/Era* likened Blazer's new business to a "street market" where "nothing will be held over night" and any remaining produce was to be "sold at special prices just before closing." The range of food sold was "traditional," as well, "from apple[s] to a crate of greens." Two weeks later, the market ran an ad in the same paper, advertising "FRESH FRUIT AND VEGETABLES DIRECT FROM THE FARM TO YOU!" The produce sold was primarily locally grown, as nearby Georgia, Tennessee, and

South Carolina farmers brought their goods to the city. While Blazer's operation was primitive in comparison with today's warehouse and lacking its multicultural focus, the market was initially successful, in part because it faced little competition from similar vendors in the local neighborhood.[7]

In the following months, the Market quietly grew and built a consumer base in the city of Decatur and in DeKalb County, but February of 1979 brought an unplanned catastrophe: a build-up of ice and snow on the roof of the building caused a collapse, causing more than $100,000 in damage. Blazer went door-to-door in Decatur to raise nearly $25,000 to aid in rebuilding the market, and dedicated customers proved critical in financing the reconstruction. "They even gave us the money to rebuild it," said Blazer. "They felt like it was their market." Upon completion, "the grateful market honored [customers'] canceled checks at the check-out counters." Blazer's brother and sister, Harry and Linda, also moved to Atlanta to help rebuild the Market and join the business, and Harry Blazer became general manager for several years.[8]

The Market's reinvention as an ethnic bazaar had its roots in these early years and was inspired not only by changing demographics but by food-industry trends as well. Throughout the 1980s, the commercial food retail industry underwent large-scale consolidation, and the massive supermarkets run by corporations such as Cincinnati's Kroger Co. placed enormous pressure on smaller, independently run firms. To survive these "supermarket wars," a business like Blazer's needed a competitive edge, which came in an expanded selection of foods unavailable in mainstream grocery stores. The Dekalb Farmers Market was one of the first groceries to experiment with internationalizing their product line, though by the end of the decade, Blazer would have a score of followers. "The revolution is now," claimed one Atlanta food writer in 1988. "Atlanta's former beans-and-potatoes complacency is being subverted by cadres of strange and alien fruits, nuts and vegetables." Growing awareness about health foods and the benefits of a varied diet contributed to the Market's popularity. In 1991 James Hood, editor of the supermarket trade publication *The Shelby Report*, praised Blazer's business as a "throwback to the old days of traditional markets." "We're seeing more of these places in response to consumer demand," he argued in an interview with the *Atlanta Journal-Constitution*.[9]

With a new location, building, and an evolving business strategy, the Market prospered as it began to attract a clientele that was quickly growing within Atlanta. The non-white and non-black population of DeKalb County nearly tripled in the 1980s, and Asian and Hispanic immigrants flocked to the market as Blazer's business began catering to this new demographic influx. Connie Siu Guinn, the daughter of two Asian immigrant entrepreneurs who opened Golden China, one of the first Chinese restaurants in nearby Snellville, remembers shopping at the Market throughout the eighties: "Going to the market was a ritual. Every Saturday my family would go. My mom would buy the produce and the products she missed so much, and my father would pick up wholesale items for the restaurant." In providing the raw materials for ethnic food vendors, the Market facilitated the operation of dozens of restaurants like the Siu Family's. The Market also became a social experience for immigrants: "I knew I would not only get a Toblerone all to myself, but that I would get to see some 'non-white' kids. Many times it was a social place too. My parents would see friends from the tightly knit Asian community." Atlanta immigrants began forming what historian Daniel Boorstin has called "communities of consumption," where "nearly all objects," certainly food, become "symbols and instruments of novel communities." These informal networks only multiplied as time passed.[10]

Thousands of shoppers swarmed the cramped aisles on weekends, and increased growth soon became problematic at the Scott Boulevard location. The food editor of the *Atlanta Journal-Constitution* quipped in 1986 that "if the three words 'Dekalb Farmers Market' leave a bad taste in your mouth, it's probably because three shopping carts pinned you in between the peppers and cucumbers one Saturday morning or a noisy, honking forklift chased you from the seafood to the cheese department." Spatial constraints necessitated a move, and in September of 1986 the Market relocated to its current location, an expanded building on East Ponce De Leon Avenue in Decatur. Designed by Robert Blazer himself, the new facility was more than four times the size of the previous location and promised "the widest, cross-cultural array of seafood, produce, deli items and baked goods ever assembled in Atlanta."[11]

At the same time, local residents near the old Scott Boulevard location, who had

The daily operation of Your Dekalb Farmers Market is one of loaded shopping carts colliding in crowded aisles, hundreds of voices speaking dozens of languages blending into a jarring cacophony inside the refrigerated warehouse, and nearly two hundred flags from all corners of the globe hanging from the rafters, perfectly reflecting the diversity of both the employees and clientele of the Market.

experienced firsthand the explosive growth of the Market and its new customer base, were happy to see it go. Despite reassurances from the DeKalb County Health Department that the Market violated no regulations, unhappy neighbors deemed it rodent-infested and malodorous; traffic flowing in and out of the market's under-sized parking lot congested city streets. "Unfounded rumors of poisonous snakes in the produce" also plagued the Market, reported an *Atlanta Journal-Constitution* writer in 1984, and it is apparent that not every Atlanta resident embraced the sudden introduction of foreign foods and cuisines into the city.[12]

A bitter family feud disrupted the operation of the Market in 1987, and Harry Blazer left the company after a personal dispute to undertake an independent venture, Harry's Farmers Markets. Eschewing the utilitarian focus and multi-ethnic clientele of his older brother's company, Harry opened stores in suburban Cobb and Gwinnett Counties, which were becoming home to middle- and upper-class, white-collar workers. Harry's Farmers Markets, while still selling products from all over the globe, had higher prices and immaculately decorated interiors that were far different from the wet concrete and fluorescent lighting of the Dekalb Market. As "the brothers are divided by their differences," reported the *Atlanta Journal-Constitution*, the two markets "divided shoppers as well." The visually pleasing Harry's Markets attracted well-to-do, native-born whites, while the Dekalb Market solidified the loyalty of its growing immigrant clientele. Many shoppers living in the suburban communities north of Atlanta stopped making the "long trip down" to Decatur, but not all believed Harry's gloss and sheen to be superior: "Harry's took the idea and made it commercial," one loyal Dekalb Farmers Market shopper insisted.[13]

Robert Blazer assured reporters that while "the appearance of the [Dekalb] Market may not be spectacular, . . . when the smoke clears, Dekalb will still be around. I don't know what will happen with these other markets." The elder Blazer was right. Though initially successful, Harry's Farmers Markets never turned a profit after 1993; the stores were eventually bought out by the natural-foods giant Whole Foods Market in 2001. "Our aspirations have exceeded our grasp because of our performance," Harry Blazer told the press after the deal was finalized. While a buy-out from a larger corporation was often financially lucrative for a smaller company, the Whole Foods deal was not negotiated entirely on Harry Blazer's terms: several of the smaller Harry's in a Hurry stores were not included in the purchase. As Harry's Markets foundered, the Dekalb Market prospered.[14]

In addition to fierce competition from Harry's and similar copycat grocery stores, the Dekalb Farmers Market faced opposition from native southerners who did not see growing multiculturalism as a positive trend. During the first Persian Gulf War in 1991, more than one hundred war veterans, opposed to the presence of an Iraqi flag among the nearly two hundred others hanging from the rafters of the relocated East Ponce Market, picketed and boycotted the store. Ten

Atlanta Veterans of Foreign Wars posts organized the demonstration in response to Blazer's refusal to remove the flag, which had been hanging inside the Market for more than three years. Reports of "harassing telephone calls, of veiled insults, and even bomb threats" alarmed market employees and shoppers, but Blazer did not yield. "We said the flags represented the people, not the politics," Blazer recalled. Many Atlantans agreed, including one who wrote a letter to the editor of the *Atlanta Journal-Constitution*: "The notion of removing an enemy's flag in time of war reminds me of an emotional teenager tearing up the photograph of an ex-boyfriend or girlfriend." While the conflict was resolved without a major boycott, it was clear that not all native Atlantans viewed the all-inclusive, immigrant-friendly market positively.[15]

Nevertheless, the flag protests, along with the earlier snake rumors and parking complaints, were isolated incidents and not representative of most Atlanta residents. The market's popularity with both natives and newcomers grew enormously over the years. "As many as 10,000 people come to shop on weekends and hundreds of others come simply to marvel at the piles of fruits and vegetables and the attendant babel of languages," wrote one *Atlanta Journal-Constitution* reporter in 1984. As Atlanta's boosters actively promoted the city's "international" status, the market became an oft-mentioned symbol of Atlanta's diversity. "If Atlanta has any claim to world-class rankings," argued one 1991 editorial, "the market boosts that claim considerably." An *Atlanta Journal* writer described the market as "Atlanta's greatest cultural melting pot," and a 1988 *National Geographic Magazine* feature on Atlanta's "energy and optimism" singled out the Dekalb Market as "something Atlantans like to brag about," as it was "an international city in itself." As many Atlanta residents enthusiastically lionized the market and incorporated it into the city's mythology, it seemed southern culture was more flexible and adaptive than previously thought.[16]

Popularity and growth brought internal problems, however, and interactions between different immigrant groups and market management occasionally proved difficult. In December 1988 eight former employees of various nationalities, both native and foreign-born, sued the Market in federal court over questionable training practices involving the "Forum," an alleged "New Age quasi-religious cult" that subjected employees to "harassment, humiliation and interrogation." In 1987 Robert Blazer joined the "human potential program" founded by New Age philosopher Werner Erhard in the early seventies. Blazer allegedly forced employees to attend group training sessions, and workers later protested that the Forum sessions violated their right to religious freedom "under the guise of 'management training.'" With eventual American Civil Liberties Union involvement, the case received significant national publicity, but was eventually settled out of court in June of 1989 by Blazer and the plaintiffs.[17]

This would not be the last dispute between labor and management: in June

1991 twenty-eight Ethiopian employees were fired for leaving work to attend a protest in Atlanta against U.S. foreign policy in their home country. A misunderstanding arose when several workers believed they had received permission to attend while Blazer denied having granted any such request. "They decided that they would much rather be at a demonstration than keep their jobs," Blazer told the press. "We love our jobs, but we love our country too," countered a former employee. Both the lawsuit and the 1991 firings demonstrated that the assimilation of immigrants into the Market's workforce was not without its problems.[18]

Despite competition, opposition, and internal division, by the mid-1990s the Market had established itself as a permanent institution for incoming Atlanta immigrants, particularly as a source of employment. "With waves of immigration, we absorb those people," Blazer said of the often-shifting workforce. "Some will stay, because they really like the business, but others will just pass through. But they get their start here: thousands and thousands of people." Welcoming refugees from around the world into its growing workforce, the Market began to assume almost a charitable, philanthropic position in the burgeoning immigrant community; an Atlanta newspaper even described Blazer as "do[ing] his small share in helping race relations." Mekonnen Yayne, an Ethiopian refugee who arrived in Atlanta in 1987 after fleeing an oppressive regime in his home country, expressed his gratitude: "I am very grateful to the Dekalb Farmers Market for the opportunity to support myself in my new life. I miss [my family] greatly, but get comfort from the family I've developed here at the Market." Each time a member from a large immigrant family was hired at the Market, he or she made possible the relocation of more relatives to Atlanta. "[Employees] send money [home], to protect their people as best they can, but as soon as they can get them over here, they do," Blazer recalled.[19]

Once in Atlanta, recent immigrants found that the wide selection of ethnic foods at the Market facilitated retention of their ethnic identities. Having moved far beyond the original apples and crate of greens, the Market became famous for its "squirming mudbugs, Morbier cheese, [and] tapioca flour," among thousands of other unusual items. Because of the Market's rapid product turnover and large clientele, Blazer has been able to order foods from all over the globe. "A guy like me can foster all this product coming in, but it's not easy to find," Blazer says. Despite this difficulty, Blazer's efforts have paid off for Juan Bautista, a Dekalb Market employee for more than twenty years and a native of Puerto Rico: "everything is here [at the Market]. No matter what country you come from, you'll always find the stuff you need." Connie Siu Guinn agrees, "You are not going to find beef tongue, tripe, fresh made samosa or rice candy at your local Kroger." Since "food was [her] parents' way to hold on to memories and pass on traditions," Connie and her family found the Market to be critical to preserving their memories, traditions, and identities.[20]

While many older immigrants clung to native foodways and shunned American mass-market hamburgers and hot dogs, their children were often drawn to the mystique of a new culture. Wendimu Abeb, a young Ethiopian who worked at the Market for two years after fleeing his homeland, admitted that he shopped at Ethiopian restaurants for a year before going to Chinese restaurants and then on to "try new things." Robert Blazer also saw younger immigrants "branching out, and start[ing to] cook different things for their families," whereas the older generation was "not going to change much." As children of immigrants forego their traditional identities, or "get caught up in the nonsense," as Bautista says, their community suffers. "They need to stay together to continue to develop their cultures." As the children of immigrants immerse themselves in mainstream American culture, the once-rigid boundaries between ethnic cuisines and cultures will continue to blur and break down.[21]

The Market was not alone in providing ethnic food to recent immigrants; Atlanta's restaurant industry experienced an explosive growth in the numbers of non-European eateries. From 92 ethnic restaurants in 1977, Atlanta in 2005 could claim 579, with nearly 200 Chinese, 162 Mexican, and more than 50 Thai restaurants. These numerical estimates may even be low, as many smaller restaurants operating with solely immigrant clienteles are not listed in the Yellow Pages. Frank Ma, a former chair of the Atlanta Chinese Restaurant Association, declared in 1995 that Atlanta had about 520 Chinese restaurants. Although Johnny Reb's Cottage and the Rebel Chef Drive-In had gone out of business, they were replaced by restaurants that blend several ethnic cuisines, such as Chico & Chang's, serving both "authentic" Mexican and Chinese food under the same roof.[22]

While Your Dekalb Farmers Market may be the largest, it is only one of many ethnic food retailers in Atlanta: equally famous is the Buford Highway Corridor, a six-mile stretch of highway that spans three counties and was home to more than seven hundred immigrant-owned businesses in 1998. This "real international boulevard," as the *Atlanta Journal-Constitution* has called it, also features a food market that is a copycat of Blazer's Decatur market, the Buford Highway Farmers Market. In addition, former Dekalb Market employees founded the nearby International Farmers Market in Chamblee, which offers similar products. As Atlanta's immigration increased over the years, more and more newcomers became food entrepreneurs, providing their compatriots with an opportunity to preserve culinary traditions.[23]

Atlanta's new ethnic restaurants and markets did not cater solely to immigrant communities: white and black southerners alike became regular shoppers and consumers of these newly introduced cuisines. As immigration historian Donna Gabaccia has noted in examining the impact of ethnic food in the early twentieth century, "enclave markets" that catered exclusively to fellow immigrants came to realize that their consumer base "provided a rather fragile financial foundation."

By reaching "beyond the boundaries of ethnic communities," immigrant entrepreneurs attempted to expand their horizons in catering to native southerners. The process was difficult at first, as rigid ethnic identities made for strictly defined tastes and preferences. "Many of my colleagues advised me not to experiment with things that were too authentic because American customers were not used to them," said a Chinese restaurant owner who arrived in Atlanta in 1977.[24]

With some adaptation by those who prepared the food and those who consumed it, cross-cultural eating became ubiquitous over time, despite initial misgivings on both sides. The "novelty, entertainment and a sense of partaking in the excitement of big city life," Gabaccia argues, drew Americans to eating outside of their traditional culture. Food consumption, as historian Andrew Heinze has noted in his examination of European Jews in America, became a "bridge between cultures," capable of signifying "one's attitude toward and place within society." Reflecting modern Atlanta's culinary mélange, John Kessler, a food writer for the *Atlanta Journal-Constitution*, described his intimate relationship with the Dekalb Farmers Market: "I love the thrilling strangeness of the place, the feeling that *this*—right here, right now—is my culture." Kessler, like many other Atlantans, is embracing Atlanta's burgeoning cultural diversity and recognizing it as his own.[25]

As immigrants from around the globe remade Atlanta into a truly international city, Robert Blazer capitalized on this nascent consumer base, and eventually the Dekalb Farmers Market became symbolic of a multicultural Atlanta. The process was neither simple nor speedy, but perfectly reflects the profound demographic changes that are giving rise to what historian Leon Fink has termed the "Nuevo

At the entrance of the Market hangs a plaque with Robert Blazer's motivational philosophy, entitled "Our Stand," which includes this pledge: We commit ourselves to the possibility this world market is for the future generations of this planet.

New South." As Atlanta lost its reputation as a city cast solely in black and white, ethnic food became the vanguard of cultural interaction, increasingly blurring the lines between foreign and native cultures and cuisines.

The history of Blazer's market also undermines the long-held popular interpretation of southern culture as reactionary, stagnant, and resistant to change. The interaction of native and foreign cultures in the last decades of the twentieth century was less of a "clash" than a slow intermingling that melded the exotic with the "down-home." Historian James C. Cobb described southern identity as "not a story of continuity *versus* change, but continuity *within* it." The same can be said for trends within foodways and ethnic cuisine, as witnessed in the eventual eagerness of Atlanta residents to experiment with their foodways. Grits and fried chicken won't disappear, but perhaps future southerners will enjoy them with a side of rice noodles or enchilada sauce.[26]

At the entrance of Your Dekalb Farmers Market hangs a plaque with Robert Blazer's motivational philosophy titled "Our Stand":

We declare the world is designed to work.

We are responsible for what does not work.

We make the difference.

No matter how technologically advanced we become, we cannot escape our fundamental relationship with food and each other. The possibility of these relationships is the world market. In this context, the world works for everyone free of scarcity and suffering.

We commit ourselves to the possibility this world market is for the future generations of this planet.

As customers of all races, nationalities, and cultures pass the sign by the thousands, I doubt that many stand in awe and contemplate the meaning of both this declaration and the larger market. But in the capital of the Sunbelt South, the quiet revolution of immigration and food continues to upset and redefine the meanings of local, regional, and global identity.

NOTES

1. Interview with Robert Blazer, 18 March 2006. I spoke with Blazer for about an hour inside his office at the market, after which he sent for two long-time employees to speak with me as well.

2. U.S. Census Bureau, *CensusCD 1980–2000* (GeoLytics, Inc., 1996–2002). "Metro Atlanta," in quoting census figures, refers to Congressional Districts 4, 5, and 6 as a representation of Atlanta and its most populous suburbs. Districts 4, 5, and 6 contain the majorities of Cobb, Fulton, Gwinnett, and DeKalb Counties.

3. Interview with Robert Blazer, 18 March 2006.

4. U.S. Census figures for DeKalb County, Congressional Districts 4, 5, 6, City of Chamblee, Georgia, 1980–2000.

5. Greater Atlanta Yellow Pages, 1977 edition, covering area code 404. In categorizing restaurants by ethnicity, I am relying completely on their names: while not 100 percent accurate, it is clear that The Golden Buddha and Frank's Ol' Home Place serve quite different entrees. I am not insisting that these numbers fully represent the number of non-European restaurants, as there may be many more that are not listed, but the Yellow Pages do provide a telling glance at the culinary atmosphere of Atlanta.

6. Herbert T. Jenkins, *Food, Fairs and Farmers' Markets in Atlanta* (Center for Research in Social Change, Emory University, 1977), 89, 84, 89.

7. *Decatur-DeKalb News/Era*, 2 June 1977; *Decatur-DeKalb News/Era*, 16 June 1977.

8. *Atlanta Constitution*, 24 June 1986; interview with Robert Blazer, 18 March 2006.

9. *Atlanta Journal-Constitution*, 15 June 1988; James Hood, *Atlanta Constitution*, 8 October 1991.

10. U.S. Census figures, DeKalb County, 1980–1990; email interview with Connie Siu Guinn, 24 March 2006; Daniel Boorstin, *The Democratic Experience* (Random House, 1973), 89–90.

11. *Atlanta Journal-Constitution*, 24–25 September 1986.

12. *Atlanta Journal-Constitution*, North DeKalb Extra, 9 October 1986; *Atlanta Journal-Constitution*, 1 July 1984.

13. *Atlanta Journal-Constitution*, Gwinnett Extra, 12 September 1993; *Atlanta Journal-Constitution*, DeKalb Extra, 9 September 1993. The details over the Blazer family feud are derived from newspaper reports only. Robert Blazer himself did not comment on the affair in our interview.

14. *Atlanta Journal-Constitution*, Gwinnett Extra, 12 September 1993; *Atlanta Journal-Constitution*, 11 August 2001.

15. *Atlanta Constitution*, 24 February 1991; interview with Robert Blazer, 18 March 2006; *Atlanta Journal-Constitution*, 21 February 1991.

16. *Atlanta Journal-Constitution*, 1 July 1984, D6; *Atlanta Constitution*, 23 February 1991, A19; *Atlanta Journal*, 15 February 1987, G7; *Atlanta Constitution*, 26 March 1991, A16; *National Geographic Magazine* 174.1 (July 1988): 3, 22.

17. *Atlanta Journal-Constitution*, 8 December 1988; quote describing the Forum as a "human potential program" comes from an article in the *Wall Street Journal*, 8 December 1988; details on suit settlement from *Atlanta Journal-Constitution*, 8 June 1989.

18. *Atlanta Constitution*, 2 June 1991.

19. Interview with Robert Blazer, 18 March 2006; *Atlanta Journal-Constitution*, DeKalb Extra, 9 September 1993.

20. "Apple[s] [and] a crate of greens" quote is from *Decatur-DeKalb News/Era*, 2 June 1977; *Atlanta Journal-Constitution*, 20 May 2001; interview with Robert Blazer, 18 March 2006; anonymous worker interview (name is fictitious) at Your Dekalb Farmers Market, 18 March 2006; email interview with Connie Siu Guinn, 24 March 2006.

21. Anonymous worker interview (name is fictitious) at Your Dekalb Farmers Market, 18 March 2006; interview with Robert Blazer, 18 March 2006.

22. Greater Atlanta Yellow Pages, 2005–2006, covering area code 404. Again, numerical counts are based on names of restaurants and occasional brief descriptions and advertisements. I did not consider large international chains such as Taco Bell to be "ethnic food" retailers and did not count them. The total number of restaurants listed in the 2005–2006 Yellow Pages was approximately 2,500; interview with Frank Ma from Jianli Zhao, *Strangers in the City: The Atlanta Chinese, Their Community, and Stories of Their Lives* (Routledge Books, 2002), 107.

23. *Atlanta Journal-Constitution*, 2 March 1998; *Atlanta Journal-Constitution*, 28 August 2003.

24. Donna Gabaccia, *We Are What We Eat: Ethnic Food and the Making of Americans* (Harvard University Press, 1998), 65; Zhao, *Strangers in the City*, 134.

25. Gabaccia, *We Are What We Eat*, 105; Andrew Heinze, *Adapting to Abundance: Jewish Immigrants, Mass Consumption, and the Search for American Identity* (Columbia University Press, 1990), 1, 8; John Kessler, *Atlanta Journal-Constitution*, 20 May 2001 (Kessler's emphasis).

26. James C. Cobb, *Away Down South: A History of Southern Identity* (Oxford University Press, 2005), 7.

Bill Smith

Taking the Heat—and Dishing It Out—
in a Nuevo New South Kitchen

with Lisa Eveleigh

Mexico and the American South share a culinary heritage as "lands of pork," and Bill Smith's Mexican kitchen staff cooks up some of the South's finest down-home specialties at the famed Crook's Corner. Photograph courtesy of Dave Shaw.

Bill Smith is the author of Seasoned in the South: Recipes from Crook's Corner and from Home *(Algonquin, 2005) and is currently writing about Mexico.*

Bill Smith is an innovative, southern-cuisine chef famous for creating such unexpected culinary juxtapositions as honeysuckle sorbet—hot summer in a cool bite. The dessert's main ingredient really is the flower, thousands of them, all gathered by hand. His peculiarly delicious tomato and watermelon salad was featured on the cover of last July's *Southern Living*. For the past fifteen years, Bill has been the head chef at Crook's Corner in Chapel Hill, North Carolina. Before that, he was chef at La Residence, a French restaurant also in Chapel Hill, where I was lucky enough to have worked in his kitchen, along with what stood for restaurant labor in the 1980s: part-time graduate students, Vietnamese immigrants, a French chef with a visa, artists, and musicians who played in the many bands that call this college town home.

Throughout the 1980s the kitchen at Crook's maintained this demographic, but in the 1990s neighbors from the deeper South began knocking at the kitchen door, ready to work. The restaurant had a few Mexican employees when Bill began working there in 1993, but he steadily hired more until, by 2000, the kitchen staff was almost entirely Latino men—thirteen out of fifteen employees. This rapid and extreme transformation of the kitchen at Crook's mirrors that of other restaurant kitchens in Chapel Hill and reflects a well-documented, overarching trend in manual labor across the South and the nation.

The deeply personal experiences of immigrants who left the large, industrial city of Celaya in the Mexican state of Guanajuato to work in the kitchens, construction sites, and landscape businesses of Chapel Hill and nearby Carrboro have been beautifully documented in *Going to Carolina del Norte: Narrating Mexican Migrant Experiences*, published by the Center for Global Education at the University of North Carolina at Chapel Hill. In this recent interview, Bill gives a name and voice to the other side of that equation: the employer, and the opportunity, waiting at the end of the long journey north. In Bill's case, his first group of workers was actually from Celaya. A few years later, a second wave of workers arrived from a remote, isolated village, Santa Maria de Ipalapa, in the state of Oaxaca. Whether from city or village, the workers find common ground once they settle in Bill's kitchen. Over the years, he has come to know his staff well, entering into their communities in Chapel Hill, traveling frequently to their homes in Mexico, always a boss, sometimes a friend, a guide, and even a sponsor in the quest for citizenship.

Twenty-five years ago, I watched Bill revel in the homemade egg rolls and shrimp soup—and gamely try the chicken feet—prepared by Mia and Hong, the Vietnamese "boat-people" who had found a safe harbor working in the kitchen at La Résidence. An anthropologist by nature, Bill collected their stories along with their recipes, and here he reveals his unique experience today as a participant observer in his own kitchen.

In Bill Smith's Words . . .

I inherited a Mexican kitchen staff when I took over the job [in 1993]. The fact of the nineties in this area was that for the wages we were able to pay, the only people who showed up to apply for jobs were from Mexico. That's how it all happened. That's how it began. I didn't go out looking for Mexicans because they were cheap.

At La Rez the kitchen was all college students and graduate students. I still had a few of those, but rarely were those people full-time. At Crook's Corner we're busy. The work can be pretty hard. I need people who are full-time—the kitchen is their principal occupation. In the early nineties, those people dried up. Whether there was more money for education or whether people found better paying jobs, those people quit coming in. Rock 'n' roll people [local band members] kept coming in, but even not so many of them.

There was a transition period where I made a decision to let the Mexican guys move on up. That was a period of Mexican dishwashers in a gringo kitchen of Americans who were—let's see, how shall I put it nicely?—who had drug problems. There was a period of substance abuse I put up with, and it was just horrible. The Mexican guys said, "Let me do it, let me do it!" and they were peerless. We showed them what to do once, and we never had to do it again. A hangover was not an excuse for missing work. A party was not an excuse for missing work. They complained about the *lack* of work, not about having to work *too much*. It was a different work ethic.

At one point, right in the beginning, I even went to the [homeless] shelter. I said, "I have *got* to have people to work." I had two people that were such horrible alcoholics that they left in two days. In the morning they were ready to work, and by four o'clock I needed to be a social worker.

I don't remember the first Mexican person I hired, but I suspect it was a friend or relative of people who were already here. If we needed a dishwasher, a cousin would come in, and it would be great because their friend that worked for me was there to say, "Okay, do this." They trained them for me, and I didn't have to worry about it. I had to fine-tune it, but it was effortless. By the end of 1999 the kitchen had transitioned to almost all Mexican. It's not like I insisted on only Mexicans at that point; they were just the consistent ones.

I have two people who have come and gone at least once, and for one of them I think it's the second time. I have a bunch of kids that showed up when they were seventeen, eighteen years old, and they are in their early twenties now. They have been here five, six, seven years now.

They come without any ego involved in it. They don't have any problem with menial work. You know how cooks can be. "No! You can't have extra salt." There's none of that at all, absolutely none of that. No matter how preposterous the request is, if it's doable, they say, "All right." And that's very refreshing, you can imagine. That's worth a lot. It takes a lot of hustle to have gotten themselves here, so I think we get the best, actually.

My workers quickly got out of [agricultural jobs]. I think that's the way you break in, because everybody was used to that. Both sides of the bargain were used to that: these compliant, acquiescent Mexicans out in the field all day. Once they were here, though, they saw other stuff. They're really go-getters. Everybody goes to every restaurant, everybody goes to every construction site, everybody goes to every landscaper—until they find work. And there always is work. I might hire a larger percentage than other restaurants, but most chefs I know hire some [Mexican] people. I share a staff that merges with 411 West, and Elmo's, and Milltown, and Acme [other restaurants in Chapel Hill-Carrboro]. We all share at least one person.

Restaurant work probably pays less than the chicken plant. I pay Mexican workers like I pay everybody else, eleven or twelve dollars an hour after they've been there awhile. You start at seven or eight dollars as dishwashers, and then you go up. I imagine some of them move up to supervisory positions in chicken plants, and those people probably make more than that. But the work is gross. I don't know what field laborers get paid apiece. There's a whole different label for that. Crook's is probably considered a good place to work. On the farms, they would have been in camps, whereas in Chapel Hill, at least, they're integrated into the town like everybody else.

They come here thinking they want to work a while and go back. And then the difficulty of going back and forth causes them to put down more roots. Then they become lonely for their families, and they get them up here somehow. And then they decide, "Well, we're here. We may as well stay." I think almost none of them come with the idea of coming to stay. Eventually they become entrenched here, but I can't think of anyone who set out to become an American. I don't think that is very typical at all.

STAY OR GO? ANTONIO AND JORGE

In the early nineties, you could come over and get yourself set up more easily and then apply for a green card. [Businesses] needed workers, it wasn't a big deal. I think it was understood, although I'm not sure why. It wasn't this wave of immigrants for one thing. It was just a few people, so it was considered okay. With the green card, if you didn't get in trouble, you were then eligible to bring your family up with you. I don't know if it was with the idea of settling permanently or temporarily, but, in any case, it could be done.

Antonio had been at Crook's longer than me, and he had a green card. He left at Christmastime [2006] because he had gotten a job at GlaxoSmithKline running the kitchen for their daycare center, which came with insurance and free school for his grandson, which of course I couldn't offer him. In the meantime, he has a house through Habitat. I'm his family's sponsor, legally on paper. Even for the ones who start out legal, it's really difficult to maneuver through the regulations and the bureaucracies, which is why so many of them throw up their hands and just sneak in. It's just too complicated. And [government is] more suspicious of everybody now [since 9/11].

In the mid-nineties another worker, Jorge, started the procedure to bring his wife and two children. He was told by immigration in Charlotte that they needed to get Social Security numbers because that would put them in the records right away. He applied, and each child got two. He didn't know why. So he came in with [the numbers] and said, "What am I supposed to do?"

I said, "Let's use the oldest number. It makes sense, that one came first."

So we submitted those with the next round of paperwork. Well, that was *not* what you were supposed to do. [laughs] It popped up as some sort of duplicity. So we would get on the phone. The immigration office in charge of his case was in Charlotte. From the minute the office opened until it closed, we got a busy signal. The only way we could get through was to start dialing before the office opened and keep hitting redial. We stood there for hours hitting redial. Finally, we would get through to somebody, but of course then they had to find the case and figure out what was going on. Sometimes the phone would just cut off. They didn't have enough people, although I have to say, the people they had were always nice. No one was ever rude to me, but I kept getting told different things. It's my experience that [migrants] have trouble with the rules or with what they're being told to do because a lot of the rules don't make any sense or they're vague. I mean, *I* had trouble with it, so if it's not your first language, then of course you would too.

Jorge was trying to obey the law. He had a green card and could go back and forth. He was going to go back home for a while. I said, "Okay, if the form comes, I'll just try to deal with it, and I'll keep it for you." When he came back, he had his wife and children.

I said, "Oh, did it all work out?"

He said, "No." [laughs]

I said, "What happened?"

He said, "Well, we could never figure out what to do, so I borrowed an ID of

"Initially everyone was from Celaya, which is in the state of Guanajuato. It's actually a really large town about the size of Greensboro [North Carolina]. It's arid, but it always feels like spring there. They even call it the 'Town of Eternal Spring.'" Bill Smith (right) and Camino, brother of a Crook's Corner employee, in Celaya during one of Smith's many visits to the town. Courtesy of Bill Smith.

someone who lives in the United States who had two babies and looked like me. I drove around Matamoras until the kids went to sleep, and then I drove across the border."

I said, "What did your wife do?"

He said, "She swam over."

They stayed for a couple of years. Again, this was all before 9/11, so nobody really cared. They had a couple more kids while they were up here. But he's gone back home now. I still get things for Jorge, and he's gone home. Every once in a while a document will come in the mail to Crook's.

He didn't want to come here to be an American. It's a big misconception: they're not all trying to come here to be citizens, although some of them may decide to live here once they've gotten here. Their kids are born here and grow up here; they want to stay. A lot of these people just want to work, and I think a movement of labor is not a bad thing. They want to be able to go back and forth, and if they could go back and forth with ease then I don't think we'd have this pile-up of people. They want to be with their families first, and if they're here working and they can't go back and forth, then the money is here.

I would use the framework of NAFTA [North American Free Trade Agreement] to make Mexico a special case and let us have a free movement of labor among the three countries [including Canada], like the European Union. You would still register people at the border and keep track of who was where and who was doing what. That would solve some of these problems: the crime syndicates on the border; the unfair labor practices that might come to pass because people are afraid of being exposed as illegals; labor shortages. People would stop coming if there wasn't work, and it would remove the uncertainty about whether there *was* work or not. When there weren't jobs, they would go somewhere else or go back home.

They would not relocate their families, and they could go back home with ease. They could go back and forth if someone was sick, if there was a funeral. I've had two people who have lost family members this year, and they couldn't get back to the funeral.

My friend Antonio, who has the house here, obviously is here to stay. He came with that in mind. I've sponsored his family for ten years now, including his worthless son. [laughs] He is less than twenty-one. He came when he was little. The kids got in a little trouble as teenagers. Antonio would say, "You have to get a job, blah, blah, blah," and his son would say, "I'm illegal. I can't do anything." When the children get to be teenagers and they realize that there's a barrier in the way—they've grown up here, but there's this barrier of illegality—then they give up. The parents are really ambitious, and the children hit this wall. They can't go to college and they can't do this and they can't do that and they just give up. They lose their motivation. That's what happened to the son. His father works really hard, always has two, three jobs. I really admire him when I think about what he has done to get his family situated. I think his son exasperates him, but he's really easy-going about it. Antonio's two daughters are not like that. They both have children now, and they have that to motivate them. I'm sponsoring them, too. Naturally, just having children makes them more responsible.

I think Jorge went back because he said the children here didn't behave. He took his back to Mexico. Antonio stayed because his [extended] family, his parents, in Mexico needed more money than he could earn down there and support his own family as well. I think that was the principal thing. And then he has children and grandchildren who mostly grew up here. I think his wife doesn't much care for it, honestly. She doesn't hate it, but I think she's always homesick—more than he.

FROM VILLAGE AND TOWN —
SANTA MARIA DE IPALAPA AND CELAYA

A lot of my workers were from the same town, although not so much now. Initially everyone was from Celaya, which is in the state of Guanajuato. It's actually a really large town about the size of Greensboro [North Carolina]. Not pretty at all—just this sprawling, run-down industrial town in the high desert. It's arid, but it always feels like spring there. They even call it the "Town of Eternal Spring."

Guanajuato is Vicente Fox's [president of Mexico 2000–2006] state, so he has brought in all kinds of development. There are all kinds of factories. It's a fairly industrialized state, but the wages in Mexico are the problem. You don't get much for your efforts.

There is a middle class there, but it's very precarious. When the peso collapsed [in 1994] the whole bottom fell out, and all these people had just clawed their way up to a middle class. Everything went to hell all of a sudden, and they had these debts with 500 percent interest on their credit cards and mortgages. The economy has come back, but there's not much trust in the institutions, although the banks are better now because of globalization—the ones that maintain international standards instead of local standards.

Angel was in that first band of people that came over that had proper papers, and they all went back to Celaya right before the peso collapsed. They had saved all this money and were going to start little businesses and do a take-out restaurant. I remember seeing them all with their cars full of televisions and stuff. They got home, and everything collapsed under them. They were back in a year and a half. They were all back.

Although Mexicans have to pay for their children's education, all my Mexican staff can read, unlike the drug abusers that worked for me. They all understand the rudiments of reading for instruction and information. Even if they don't speak the language, I can put a recipe before them and tell them what those words mean, and they can do what it says. This is true for everyone. I have kids from Oaxacan villages that are very primitive, and they all can read. Oaxaca's a little different, though. There is a great respect for education in that state.

Usually their English is okay when they arrive—basic. I have probably done them a disservice by speaking Spanish all the time instead of making them speak English. Now I don't think about what language I'm speaking. I go back and forth all the time. I just start talking and whatever language comes out, comes out. It's more efficient, really, for me to speak Spanish. Sometimes they talk so fast I can't figure out what they're saying, but most of the time I can understand everything.

I speak a very coarse version of Spanish—Mexican street Spanish, I'm told. They teach me terrible things [laughs] that I would never say in English. I've been told on more than one occasion, "Don't talk like that in front of my mother!"

After I have met their mothers, I'll say, "How did I do?"

And they'll say, "Okay. You only did one thing bad, and that was all right." [laughs]

Not everybody in the kitchen is from Celaya now. My main line cook is from Puebla, which is known for its universities, and people from Puebla are sort of snooty about it. I've noticed this all over Latin America, but it's true in Mexico, particularly, that there is great pride in their old universities and their traditions of learning. Even people who are not intellectuals respect people who consider themselves to be intellectuals. There is a respect for education that I don't see here, at least not generally. There is a great respect for learning, even among the people who know they can never be educated.

Some of the workers from Celaya knew each other there, but not all did. When they got up here they connected. I hired the cousin of the guy from Puebla and some of his friends. Two years ago, I went to the wedding of the kid from [Santa Maria de Ipalapa, a village in] Oaxaca. He's back. He's working for me now. I had thirteen cousins up here together from that village, and when I went back for the wedding I knew all these people in that village. They hadn't all worked for me, but I had met them. The wedding was five hours by bus, and then two hours by car out of the city of Oaxaca, way up in the mountains. I didn't realize how remote it was, and so I had only given myself a long weekend. I stayed a day, basically, in the village.

The water system there was quite mysterious. Toilets were hooked into some sort of sewer system, but I think it went into the river, where everyone was bathing, which I did not do. I had to be really careful, because you can't be on a bus for seven hours with one of those third-world intestinal things. My whole motivation the entire time I was up in the mountains was "Do not eat vegetables. Do not use ice cubes. Do not drink water." So I drank beer all the time, which was fine.

The Mexicans dote on their children. They're always looking out for their children's lot. The children in Santa Maria were so spoiled and happy and well-dressed, even though it's a poor place. Just millions of them everywhere, well-behaved, but loud and boisterous. For this wedding, everyone was in their finest clothes, and it was just as sweet as could be. It must have been a struggle to buy those party dresses for these little girls, but everybody had them. It was important to them, and they were proud of it.

You don't see the lazy or mentally ill. This village was really poor, but there weren't beggars on the streets. Their families were looking after them. When I was there, everybody had come from everywhere for this wedding. There was this gaggle of old drunk uncles under a tree in the backyard. They were so drunk I couldn't understand anything they said because they were switching into an Indian dialect. But people just said that that was their cross to bear, over there under the tree.

There were no more than three thousand people in the town, although it was pretty hard to judge, and most of them were at that wedding party that night. Everything was cooked out in the yard on fires, and in big cauldrons there were chiles rehydrating in water. It was quite a production.

There was an internet cafe in town, very rudimentary, but it had glass in its windows to keep the dust out, unlike the other houses. You go in and rent the computer by the hour. You can buy beer and ice and Cokes. People have little rooms in their homes that are like stores. You see this all over Mexico. My friend Rigoberto, his wife sells shoes. She has an inventory of shoes that he built up while he was here, and it was like a little shoe store, a tiny little room. There's no other place to buy shoes nearby, so I guess she gets to sell all the shoes. That generates a little cash for them.

My workers were always homesick for this little village, and my first impression was "This is a shanty town!" I had always heard that all the cousins lived on the same street and would do stuff together. They pick a certain fruit at a certain time

"There was a transition period where I made a decision to let the Mexican guys move on up. The Mexican guys said, "Let me do it, let me do it!" and they were peerless. We showed them what to do once, and we never had to do it again. They complained about the lack of work, not about having to work too much. It was a different work ethic." In the kitchen at Crook's Corner, courtesy of Bill Smith. The employee on the right has come and gone from Celaya to Crook's three times.

of year. They slaughter the hogs at a certain time. On the river, they fish, and there are these freshwater shrimp and all that kind of thing. I always thought it was this idyllic village. Then I got there, and it was so run down, with mud streets and corrugated shacks. I couldn't connect what I had heard with what I was seeing.

After a day there, I understood. They had a hard life, but it was a very good life. Most of the people I know were not destitute and desperate. They were like the working poor [here]. They could have gotten by like they were, for the most part. It would always be a struggle, but it would be doable. But people want something better, and once they tap into something better, they can't just go back. They're not being let alone now; the rest of the world is coming in to intrude. The people who depend on these [migrant workers] get used to a higher standard of living. The system is starting to break up, starting to falter. When the workers go back home, when all this money is not coming in anymore, even though they are fine—they have homes and they have enough to eat—they have gotten used to having more cash and they become dissatisfied. They're just caught between two different worlds.

A lot of the workers have gone back to this little village. A couple of them got in trouble with the law for drunk driving, so they couldn't stay [in North Carolina]. They see themselves as failures now because they are not generating all this income anymore. I saw some of my older friends there, and I'm worried about them. There is hardly any way to make any money in that town. Only the teachers get paid—this *is* Oaxaca. But people farm, there is enough food, the houses are fine, the sanitation is okay. Everybody has livestock, and everybody knows how to butcher animals. But now the people there are used to having more cash coming in. In some ways it is really good, but now that they have tapped into the outside world, it's not going to suit. It's the global economy, and they're pawns in this. These are forces beyond anything they can control.

REGION, RACE, AND PREJUDICE

The South and Mexico are lands of pork. They put lard in everything. Every town I've ever been in Mexico has a *chicheroneria* store, which is a store that sells only pork rinds. And there *are* different kinds. There are different degrees of crispness, and skinned or unskinned, meaning the hard part on the outside is left on. Sometimes they are pickled, white and vinegary, like pickled pigs' feet, which I don't care for very much.

My workers like most southern food, although they don't like vinegar, oddly. They'll eat those pickled *chicheroneria*, but most of the time they can't stand vinegar. But they'll eat a lemon or a lime like an apple. They like black-eyed peas and rice; that's beans and rice, to them. Here, they like greens, although I don't recall seeing that in Mexico. Mexican food is varied. It is much more regional than we are, so within Mexico, what is food in one place is strange in another. They go to Mexican restaurants here, but not *just* Mexican restaurants. They love those big Vietnamese phos [stews]—all this gristle floating in broth, which is what the food in Mexico is like. [laughs]

Those little Mexican grocery stores are great. When I'm going to somebody's house, I'll pick up stuff to take. There's a certain kind of Mexican pastry that they just love. It's not very sweet but brilliantly colored with strange, interesting shapes. I call it a privation pastry because once they couldn't afford much sugar, but they developed a taste for it. Even though they could afford sugar now, they still like it because they remember it. A lot of southern foods started out the same way.

The mango salad we do [at Crook's] I learned in Mexico, and there's clearly an upping of the hot pepper flakes in the collards and things. But that is as much the public's tastes as anything. The public's taste has definitely shifted considerably and quickly.

I'm not sure if the Mexicans have a concept of the United States in a regional way or not. They have a concept of life in the big cities, and so the contrast to that is obvious. Almost everyone has a relative either in New York or Chicago or Los Angeles. They know what Mexico City is like. They see the difference between those big urban areas and the [American] South. And they're very much aware of race.

The race thing in Mexico is much different. It's still based on skin color, dark to light, but it is all dark to light shades of *brown*. Light is better. Vicente Fox looks like a European.

An insult to someone is to say *"indio,"* meaning "Indian," even though they are all dark. It's not like "nigger." It's not mean like that; it doesn't have any hate attached to it. It's just a put-down, an assumption of less intelligence, less sophistication. I have seen somebody's feelings get hurt from being called an *indio*. But, on the other hand, they call each other *"moro"* all the time, and that means "Arab," which they got through Spain, because there are hardly any Arabs in Mexico. But that's not really an insult; it's like in rap music when they call each other "nigger." It's an affectionate thing, almost. The slang changes constantly. It evolves just like American English.

Individually, the Mexicans I know get along with blacks here in North Carolina. But a lot of them have lived in really bad neighborhoods, and most of the crimes [they experience] are perpetrated by black teenage boys or men. So there's a real general prejudice in that regard. This prejudice isn't an active prejudice, it's a wary prejudice. The initial impression they get when they first get here is that these people are dangerous to them, but when they get to know black people individually, it's not an issue.

Mexicans are known to carry a lot of cash until they learn the system, and they are easy hits for robbery. At first, they would just rent the cheapest places they could find, which were in poor neighborhoods, and here that is often where black people live. They are fairly open and friendly people, so they were easy marks. People would stop them on the street and say, "Give me your money," and they would! It used to happen all the time, but it doesn't happen so much now. You can transfer funds quickly and easily now, which could not be done when they first got here.

They don't really grasp why race in this country is what it is. They don't see that. They have no history of it. The slavery in Mexico involved Indians. You never see black people in Mexico, so it is not really an issue in the way it is here. It doesn't go back as deeply, and it doesn't interject itself everywhere.

My kitchen staff bring their prejudices with them, but I disabuse them of it because I treat everybody the same and I make them do it, too. It's clear that the Pueblans look down on the Oaxacans, and that the Oaxacans would expect them to. It's all part of the set piece. But, like I said, once they become friends, it isn't so much of an issue.

There is a general lack of self-confidence among Mexicans that I have found startling. I drove to Mexico with a kid from Celaya, and on this side of the border he could not wait to get back. As soon as we got into Mexico, all of the shortcomings of society there became apparent, and he kept saying, "Oh, this is Mexico, what do you expect?"

I kept saying, "Stop saying that! It's so self-defeating. You don't have to put up with anything." But they do, because they have. You know—the corrupt police that we paid off, as we made our way down.

AT HOME IN THE NORTH

As far as public services go, my workers are real careful that they don't seem to be freeloading. The only time that they will step over that line is when their children are sick, and they take them to the hospital. My argument is that anyone at that wage level with a family is going to need public assistance in some ways wherever they are from, particularly medical. Nobody can afford that. Say it's an American person with four children making that wage; they are still going to have to have help. People say they are draining the medical system, but anybody at their wage-level would be draining it, one way or the other.

They go to the schools, but they are paying taxes here. They are paying taxes. And they are paying Social Security. You have to pay Social Security, even if you don't do any withholding or anything. They are never going to see it. In fact, that might be a real shock if they actually ever did round them all up and send them away—all that money suddenly not coming into Social Security.

My workers now live in apartment buildings that are almost all Latino. They are affordable, and the rules about how many people can live in a place seem to be lax. I would say five people live in a two-bedroom place. I have been to many Mexican homes, and you have no expectation of any kind of privacy, even with the middle-class people I know. Somehow, when I visit, I always get my own room—even though nobody has a room—because I am a guest. But being crowded in a small apartment is not considered a privation of any sort.

There have been robberies in the apartments. Another friend named Antonio, who was here for seven years, didn't want to leave his money in his apartment, but he didn't like carrying it around either. I took him down to the bank, and I explained to the woman that he wanted an account and he needed two ATM cards so his wife could access his money with her card in Mexico and he'd have his here. [The banker] said, "Okay, how much money do you have?" He took it out, and it was thirteen thousand dollars. I thought she was going to have a stroke. [laughs] I had no idea he had been walking around with thirteen thousand dollars in his pocket all the time. That would have been a calamity if he had gotten robbed. Imagine! Years of work and all that gone. Antonio bought a house [in Celaya], bought two buses and had a little bus company going. But he's back in Florida, putting down marble floors in Tampa. He still has one bus and his cousin runs it. But they have four children . . . .

I made all my workers go get bank accounts and ATM cards. In the beginning,

I went through this whole thing where everybody's postal money orders were robbed out of the post offices in Mexico and cashed. They sent postal money orders by regular mail, which were insured, but to get the money back took a lot of effort. After they got bank accounts, Antonio was mailing [local] power bills and stuff like that. I said, "Write your check. You can put it in this envelope, and you can put it in the mailbox."

He said, "Do I leave it there?"

I said, "Yes." [laughs]

He felt like he had to sit there and wait until they came and got it to make sure it was going to be safe. A mailbox on the corner! There are parts of Mexico where it is very efficient and everything works, and some parts where nothing does. The states are really autonomous, and their traditions are different. Querétaro is a tiny state in northeast Mexico known for being clear and orderly and well-run and safe. People there would probably put the mail in the mailbox and not think about it, but in Celaya they didn't.

Now there is actually a company, Vigo [Remittance Corp.], that does money transfers. All the Mexican stores have these big signs saying "Vigo," and there's one everywhere in Mexico. It's safe, it comes with a pin number. You go to a computer terminal and type it in and get a receipt. Then you call the bank in Mexico and give the number they need to the teller at the other end. But they also use the ATM cards too. It's actually less expensive, and it's more immediate.

MEN AND WOMEN

There are teenage boys everywhere, in any culture. One of my workers was trying to strike up a conversation with a waitress by calling her "short stuff." She was busy, and she didn't give him the time of day. In Mexico, a term of endearment is *chaparita*, meaning, basically, "little short girl." That is not a compliment in English—you are telling someone they are small and short—but the Mexicans see it as dainty, ladylike and dainty. Personal observations are not appreciated in this culture, in general, but in Mexico, and probably in this culture at one time, too, that was the initial introductory banter. You would make superficial comments about the other person, hoping to get their attention or start a conversation. Waitresses have complained, but we are in the second or third round of people [cycles of immigrant groups within the restaurant] here now, so the word is out. The workers know. They don't see why we have these boundaries, but they know they are there. I used to have to take people outside and say, "Now, listen! You're going to get in trouble. There are laws about this."

Their first reaction would be, "What about freedom of speech? You're always going on about freedom of speech in this country. What is this?"

I said, "Well you can't hassle people at work. It's never okay to bother people, freedom of speech or not."

And they said, "Well, you know, you're actually talking out of both sides of your mouth." [laughs]

They would never grab or touch people inappropriately, but they would say, "Ah, mamacita!" and that kind of stuff. In Mexico, that's considered complimentary. I said, "Well, people here just think you're dumb." They don't believe me.

They said, "They might think *you're* dumb when *you* do it, but when *I* do it they know it's a compliment."

There is some cross-cultural dating, but Mexican men want to be the boss and it almost never works out, although there are notable exceptions. Antonio Rodriguez, who is also from Celaya, married the publicist from Algonquin [Press], and they are very happy. I'm not sure how they met. I think she liked to go salsa dancing. That's where the real interaction is.

I think these Mexicans guys are actually really hot when they are young, and I think these college girls like them for a while, although they don't see it as a long-term thing. I had one Mexican boy, René, whose heart was absolutely broken by a gringa, absolutely broken. He thought, "This is it." Then she was off to France for a year abroad. They met at one of those salsa clubs. They had been together about six months. She was a student, full-time and serious, and he was this really cute kid. He would come in to work and say, "I'm crazy with love." He would say that every day.

I would say, "I just don't feel good about this."

But you can't give people that kind of advice. They don't want to hear it. That's why he was "crazy" with love.

Her father came to town and had to have a talk with him. I think she was very wealthy, a very well-heeled New Englander. Her father came to get her ready to go to France for the year, and René expected to be included in all these plans. Apparently it was quite a somber dinner. He was real sweet, but he ended up getting in lots of trouble after that. He ended up in jail. He just went crazy. He is back home now, has a girlfriend, and all that stuff passed. He was lonely. He couldn't have been nineteen. I don't think she realized how seriously he would take it—a whole different point of view. Mexican men like the idea that there are loose women around [laughs], but they don't want it to be anyone they know. That's probably not that different from anywhere else.

Married workers may play around, they may not. There's not anybody to play around with, really, except the college girls that come to salsa dancing. I think there is an unspoken agreement. The wife doesn't want to know, although she sort of expects it, but I'm not sure it's that different from any other society. They never talk about their exploits. You would hear more about it in a high-school

"A lot of these people just want to work, and I think a movement of labor is not a bad thing. They want to be able to go back and forth, and if they could go back and forth with ease then I don't think we'd have this pile-up of people." Photograph courtesy of Hannah Gill.

locker room. A lot of the hitting on women they do because they're showing off for the other guys, not because they're interested in the women. They're strutting in front of the other guys. The success is not necessarily the issue. The form is what counts, the ritual.

In Mexico, the long marriages I've seen start out with the man in charge and end up with the woman in charge. You don't much see a sharing of responsibility and power. I've noticed they feel you have to get married, so often they marry early on, because they're supposed to, and then later they discover maybe they should not have married that person, or gotten married at all, or should have waited. There's not much divorce, so they put up with whatever situation they are in. Usually, if it's an old couple together, they have worked it all out and are fairly content. But up here the younger people now are exposed to other things. I know one person that divorced once they got up here and two instances of somebody's getting somebody pregnant up here.

[The incentive to have a child born in the States] is in the news a lot. I don't think they ever intend to do that, but once they feel settled here they start having children. I don't think people really think that when the child turns eighteen they can sponsor their parents to come back. It's not really a motivation to have children.

Anyplace where the men and women are treated equally is a prosperous country, with some exceptions. Some of the oil countries are so wealthy that people are better off no matter what—that's a fluke. But if you go to Europe or Scandinavia or Canada, the more equal the women, the better the economy. It's just a given. What happened in Chile needs to happen in Mexico. That will make a big difference there. And it is happening. Actually, it didn't happen quickly here. Mexico now reminds me of growing up in the fifties in the South. After dinner all the women would go in the kitchen and wash dishes, and all the guys would go on the porch and talk about sports. When I was growing up, that was the way it was. The father had the last word and all that stuff.

[In Mexico] the women stand at the back of the table. There's deference, and there's a doting on the first son that's way beyond what ought to go on. The first boys are all just spoiled, even in the poorest families. I remember things like that growing up that are no longer the case in this country. The fathers probably acquiesce, but it is the mothers that do this. It's sad in a way. I have [Mexican] friends who have very smart daughters who clearly get second-hand attention.

The station of the women in Mexico is improving pretty rapidly at this point. Maybe not in the farthest corners of the country, but the consciousness is there. I was there a few years ago during the Athens Olympics, and we were watching them. The two Mexican medal winners were both women, a cyclist and a runner. I happened to make a remark in the home of one of my friends who had two college-aged daughters. I said, "Isn't it neat that all the medalists from Mexico were women this year?" All the girls said, "Yes!" and [laughs] all the men got so uncomfortable. So there's a stirring there.

Mexico's in a state of societal flux. Mexicans are very observant, and I think they will pick up the things from us they see as beneficial. I think that things will change as the country becomes a little bit more . . . more mixed up, and the cultures move back and forth more. I think that will happen. That will be good for Mexico. It will be really good for Mexico, actually.

Of Chickens and Men

Cockfighting and Equality in the South

by Marko Maunula

"Hundred on the black cock! Hundred on the black cock!"

"Fifty-forty on the red!"

"Fifty-forty, red! You and me, okay?"

Two handlers holding colorful gamecocks enter the arena, and the crowds at the Bayou Club in Vinton, Louisiana, start yelling their bets. The audience greets the birds—two large and beautiful roosters, stripped of their wattles and combs—with excited noise. Loud betting and encouragement accompany the roosters' entry to the center of the pit, a small, sandy coliseum surrounded with wire fence and Plexiglas.

Inside the pit, the handlers, a Hispanic man sporting a Stetson and a wiry young Caucasian with a soft south Louisiana accent, shake hands and let their roosters take a quick peck at each other. The birds struggle to get loose, each eager to assault the cock that has entered its space and consciousness. At the referee's signal, the handlers let their roosters go, and the birds, as if filled with sacred rage, assault each other in a hurricane of feathers, beaks, glittering spurs, and flapping wings. The fight is almost too fast and furious for the eyes to follow. After less than two minutes of intense fighting, the black cock leaps in the air, slams his razor-sharp steel spur deep into the chest of the other bird, jerking to release his weapon from the opponent. The wounded bird takes a couple of stuttering steps before falling dead on the sand.

As the black rooster parades victoriously in the pit, people in the stands settle their bets, walk to the concession stands for another beer and a cigarette, joke and discuss the fight they just witnessed. Despite the betting and the corresponding adrenaline, the atmosphere is jovial, shaped by friendly banter and a moderate flow of Budweiser. It is early Saturday evening in Louisiana, and the derby is about halfway through. It will take at least twenty more fights before the winner of the weekend's tournament—and the hefty multi-thousand dollar purse—is settled.

The crowd gathered at the cockfight offers a demographic snapshot of the contemporary, blue-collar rural South. Whites, a few African Americans, Asians, and numerous Hispanics sit scattered in the Bayou Club's ascetic stands. Hispanic influence is now a visible presence in the arena. Spanish has replaced Cajun French as the most dominant minority language. At the sales stands by the exits,

They defended their game with passion, with oft-repeated and well-rehearsed arguments that soon became familiar. Cruelty? "Our fowl is much better taken care of than those chickens you eat at KFC." Photograph courtesy of Superbass, Wikimedia Commons, under the GNU Free Documentation License.

peddlers of cockfighting paraphernalia have added Hispanic trinkets alongside the ubiquitous T-shirts, baseball caps, and other traditional sales stand favorites. This mixing of people and influences reflects cockfighting's role in southern tradition, at least here in Louisiana, the last southern state where the game remains legal. Even today, the pit serves its historical function as a cultural middle ground, a meeting point and melting pot of southern subcultures, ethnic groups, and economic classes. Today, it is an important avenue of interaction for rural white southerners and the region's Hispanic newcomers, whose presence reflects the game's popularity in Mexico and parts of Central America, as well as these cockers' desire to keep their hobby even in their new country.

Cockfighting is, by its nature, a semi-clandestine game practiced by an almost fraternal group of enthusiasts who carefully control access to the pits. Gaining entrance to the group would be the first challenge. Hailing from Finland, I couldn't be more of an outsider, yet, my curiosity sparked, I accepted the assignment when a Finnish magazine asked me to write about this peculiar game that still survived in parts of the South. My entry to the cockfighting circles was the result of long and arduous footwork. After weeks of unanswered emails and a desperate search for contacts, Bobby Jones, a friendly Texan, promised to help with the story and host me and a photographer at a cockfighting derby in Louisiana. Jones belongs to a new school of cockfighters who had come to the realization that only publicity could save their game from further legislative assaults. These cockers believed that the old strategy of continuing the game in silence and hoping that animal-rights activists and other moral crusaders would simply go away was doomed. As a result, Jones and his friends have devised a new media strategy focused on sharing their stories with writers who might be more sympathetic toward — or at least not strongly biased against — their game.

We met in Vinton early in the summer of 2004. After a day of casual talking, sharing a couple of beers, and dining on chicken gumbo, Jones and the owner of the Bayou Club became convinced that these two blond Scandinavians were neither scandal-searching muckrakers nor undercover PETA agents. After we promised that we would not take photos inside the arena and that we would respect the privacy of individuals who did not want to talk to us, we were invited to the pits.

Once we were accepted into the circle, we found most cockers to be very hospitable, friendly men eager to talk about their roosters. They defended their game with passion and oft-repeated, well-rehearsed arguments that soon became familiar. Cruelty? "Our fowl is much better taken care of than those chickens you eat at KFC. We pamper our chickens with free-range living and good feed." Crime and negative side-effects? "If we find it, we deal with it. Today's cockfighting is clean." Why cockfighting? What kick do you get from watching two birds have a go at each other? "It's exciting, and it's our tradition, an old southern game."

Cockfighting *is* quite possibly the South's oldest game. Many of the region's first settlers and explorers, starting with Sir Walter Raleigh himself, were well-known cockfighting enthusiasts. The height of the game's popularity in England, during the reigns of Elizabeth I and James I, coincided with the establishment and growth of Britain's southern colonies.[1] Gamecocks entered the South simultaneously with African slaves, the plantation economy, socially ambitious Englishmen, and other fundamental building blocks of the emerging southern culture.

While cockfighting had its fans in all British North American colonies, the game's most enthusiastic aficionados could soon be found in the South, and historical records indicate that it was widespread in the antebellum era. The pits became important centers of socialization and entertainment in the often isolated, socially deprived South. Southern men throughout the region met at the pits to make bets, exchange gossip, and share drinks, as well as fight their roosters. The violent game, with its strict honor code and emphasis on bravery, seemed tailored to southern tastes.[2]

The pits also offered opportunities for interracial and interclass socialization in the Old South. Although close interaction between whites and blacks was often a daily reality in the antebellum South, the pit, with its small and intimate environs, offered a distinctively unique forum for interracial dealings. The ethos of gambling, its obsessive nature, the relative unpredictability of cockfighting, and, finally, outsiders' hostility toward the game made the cockfighting brotherhood a close-knit circle. The thickest lines separating insiders and outsiders were drawn—then as well as now—between the pit and the outsiders, not inside the pit itself. The surviving documents and articles about cockfighting, such as *Harper's New Monthly Magazine*'s May 1857 illustrated article, show the racially and economically diverse character of the antebellum pit, with the crowds ranging from poor slaves and poor whites to planters and other members of social prominence. The lust for this blood sport drew mostly moral—not economic or racial—lines across the southern communities.[3]

Cockfighting is quite possibly the South's oldest game. Many of the region's first settlers, starting with Sir Walter Raleigh himself, were well-known cockfighting enthusiasts. Gamecocks entered the South simultaneously with African slaves, the plantation economy, socially ambitious Englishmen, and other fundamental building blocks of the emerging southern culture. Cockfighting at General Orlando B. Wilcox's headquarters in Petersburg, Virginia, 1864, courtesy of the Collections of the Library of Congress.

Throughout most of its history in British North America, cockfighting has been a controversial game. The moral arguments for and against the practice are nothing new, although nowadays most objections focus more on the welfare of the animals than on gambling or the game's corrupting effects on the human participants, like most of the early criticisms did. As early as the Revolutionary Era, the leaders of the Wilmington Jockey Club, a major North Carolina gamecock association, expressed concern that the Continental Congress was possibly casting a critical eye toward "gaming, cock-fighting . . . and other expensive diversions and entertainments." Cockfighting was a game of barely controlled passions, extraordinary gambling, and thoroughly anti-Puritan behavior—all served in the framework of appropriate gentility to make it acceptable for socially aspiring southern planters.[4]

The derision of outsiders and the resulting clannishness of the cocker community cut not only across time periods but also geographic boundaries. Anthropologist Clifford Geertz, for example, recounts how the Balinese community that he set out to study fully accepted him only after he attended an illegal cockfight that culminated in an eventful escape from the raiding police force.[5] The game's inclusiveness is mostly a reflection of the ingroup-outgroup dynamics that often tie members of an oppressed or deviant group together, resulting in a close-knit and cohesive community, regardless of the participants' social status outside the group. This continues to be decisively true, especially in the contemporary South.

The pit itself, as a physical venue, has very little value as a center of relaxation or entertainment. A crude and malodorous building that is barely more than a glorified warehouse, Vinton's Bayou Club is nevertheless one of the more attractive pits around.[6] In Louisiana, where all kinds of gambling is legal, the opportunity simply to place *illegal* bets is not itself an effective lure either. In addition to the opportunity to see scores of roosters kill each other, the men are drawn by the strong, if temporary, sense of community. The physical unattractiveness of the pit, the concession stand's cheap and limited menu, and the bare, undifferentiated seating impose the equality of discomfort on all participants. This bonding contributes to the closeness of the community and sense of equality and camaraderie inside the pit, which is further enforced by the restrictive entry policies. Only cockers are welcome. The owners of the clubs usually keep a close eye on the door, barring the entry of those who do not look like cockers or might have a negative view of the goings-on inside the pit. The group gathered in the Bayou Club is, quite literally, a hand-picked community, united in spirit and in a very real and tangible membership in the club, for which each person in attendance paid forty dollars.

Cockfighting in America today is still a decidedly southern game. Some northern states, such as Massachusetts and Pennsylvania, banned the sport even before the Civil War, while in the South the game continued to be legal well into the twentieth century. Cockfighting is now legal only in Louisiana, where betting on the fights already is illegal, as will be the sport itself in 2008. Illegal fights are commonplace throughout the South, though, especially in parts of Appalachia and the heavily Hispanic counties of southern Texas. In popular cockfighting regions, the laws against the game are often dead letters, largely not enforced. Political campaigns for sheriff's offices or other law enforcement positions often contain privately whispered promises of continuing the truce between local cockers and law enforcement.[7]

Even though the game is illegal, gamecock farms spot the landscape across the rural South from Virginia to Texas. Especially in Appalachia and rural Louisiana, even a casual visitor can spot the occasional field full of individual shelters, with leash-bound roosters guarding these small fiefdoms complete with harems of hens. A dedicated cocker must breed scores of roosters in a year in order to have enough birds for the long, nine-month tournament season. While a handful of exceptionally successful cockers can make a substantial living by breeding and fighting their fowl, or by manufacturing and selling feeds, spurs, and other cockfighting tools, for the majority of the participants, cockfighting is an expensive and time-consuming hobby. Breeding and training gamecocks takes research and backbreaking labor. Most cockers, despite their lack of formal training, have acquired impressive knowledge of genetics, feeding, fowl health and diseases, training, and other factors necessary to breeding particularly powerful, aggressive, and, therefore, victorious gamecocks. Jim Demoruelle, a veteran cocker from Ville Platte, Louisiana, notes that many breeders practically live on their farms, tending to their chickens with the latest expensive feeds and medications, studying breeding charts, and exercising their combatants.

Cockers attribute this dedication to the obsessive, addictive nature of the game. Some cockers argue that attending cockfights is a harder habit to kick than smoking or heavy drinking. "I call it the three-fight rule," says Demoruelle: "If you visit three cockfights, you get hooked." Demoruelle, an intelligent man with a long career in running drug and alcohol abuse rehabilitation clinics, demonstrates obvious signs of the addiction that afflicts thousands of dedicated gamecock enthusiasts.

"Most cockers are smart, but not necessarily very socially skilled or verbally expressive people," Demoruelle observes, matter of factly. "For the most part, they live in isolated, rural areas, and they don't always develop good social skills. However, when it comes to their roosters, they have acquired an impressive knowledge of their game fowl, with very complex understanding of the principles of genetics. You cannot be successful in this sport without extensive work and knowledge."

The dedication of cockers and the time-consuming, often socially isolating preparation required of cockfighting have emphasized the pit's role as the focus of cockers' lives. Cockers have turned increasingly inwards as the game has faced increased legal and ethical pressure from state and federal legislatures, animal-rights activists, antigambling interests, and a general public that often views this blood sport as a dying relic from the bad old days. Rarely verbal in defending their game to start with, most cockers have become even more withdrawn, fiercely private and reluctant to talk about their obsession to the outsiders.

"Some of us have given in on the pressures," says Bobby Jones, the Texas cocker who helped me gain entrance to the Bayou Club pit. "I haven't. I am proud of my hobby. There is nothing wrong with cockfighting." Jones appreciates the social aspects of spending weekends in the pits, in the company of fellow connoisseurs, in a place where nothing needs an explanation or an apology: "The best part of cockfights is the friendship, getting together with other cockers."

With entry to cockpits limited and an insider-outsider ethos pervasive, fellow cockers are accepted and appreciated, usually regardless of their ethnic or economic backgrounds.[8] The crowd consists of working-class southerners—white, African American, Asian, and Hispanic—with a few successful businessmen and other entrepreneurs thrown into the mix. Women are a noticeable minority—with a very few exceptions, cockfighting is a man's business. And judging by the license plates on the Bayou Club's parking lot, weekend-long derbies in places like Vinton, Louisiana, attract hundreds of enthusiasts all over the South, from North Carolina to Texas and the states in between.

Although minorities are largely well received in the cockpits, many of the cockers do not necessarily demonstrate a consistently enlightened disposition toward outsiders or people from different cultures and ethnicities, yet in the pits the dy-

In his seminal essay on cockfighting in Bali, anthropologist Clifford Geertz recounts how the Balinese community that he sets to study fully accepts him only after he attends an illegal cockfight, culminating in an eventful escape from the raiding police force. Winning cock and owner at the completion of a cockfight in Bali in 2004, photographed by VJM, courtesy of Wikimedia Commons, under the GNU Free Documentation License.

namics of the game and the derision of the outsiders tie the participants together. "When cockfighters come together, they do not discuss where somebody is from or how much money they have. They only talk about chickens," says Jim Demoruelle. Especially considering the rural, working-class character of contemporary cockfighting in the South, for many participants the pit has created a unique forum where their predominant notions about cultural demarcations blur, at least temporarily. The pit forms an ethnic-reality distortion bubble of sorts, where cockers' views of each other are reduced to their lowest common denominators: regardless of the accent or complexion, they are all first and foremost cockers. The community is too small and too threatened by outsiders for ethnic division or other types of clannishness to dominate the atmosphere and, therefore, to divide the crowd.

A man's status or reputation as a cocker can elevate him in the eyes of some racially less enlightened participants. One Mississippi cocker admits openly that he does not particularly care for African Americans: "I don't hate them, but I don't really seek their company. They do their thing, I do mine. I am not a racist, just a southerner." However, Roy Jones Jr., perhaps the greatest boxer of the last decade and an avid cockfighting enthusiast who visits derbies periodically, receives nothing but praise from the Mississippian: "Roy is the nicest man. He comes to the derbies, watches the fights, talks about the roosters. He is just one of the crowd, not making a show of himself."

The Mississippian's comment reveals the contradiction in cockfighting's inclusiveness. While the inclusiveness of the hobby is quite real and the dynamics of the pit enforce an aura of equality, the social circle that is born inside the pits is a deviation from many participants' openly xenophobic and racist attitudes in the larger world. The Mississippi cocker's views reflect a very exclusive understanding of what it is to be a southerner, with more than a whiff of the ugly mindsets of yore. Paradoxically, an old, bloody, and brutal southern game, surviving on the fringes of the region's culture, offers him a temporary and narrow bridge to create a more modern, normal, and egalitarian connection to his fellow African American southerners. As far as racial attitudes are concerned, cockfighting drags him, at least temporarily, into the twenty-first century.

Hispanics especially have been welcomed into the circle warmly. If anything, many native southerners who have gathered in the pit seem mildly and politely curious about the Hispanic participants, often consciously working to make them feel welcome in the pits. Hispanic cockers, sometimes operating on a stricter budget than more established native participants, receive kudos for their guts and dedication from their English-speaking colleagues. "At first Mexicans were easy wins in the tournaments. They didn't necessarily have the latest knowledge on training, feeds, and breeding. Now, they are learning. Mexicans are getting better all the time," Bobby Jones nods approvingly.

The atmosphere in the pit is showing growing Hispanic influence. The rhythms of *Norteño* music pumping from the car stereos parked outside the pit, Mexican cowboy outfits, the peddlers of cockfighting paraphernalia, and the ever present Spanish language all offer evidence of the growing Latin influence in the pits. Some cockers even see the arrival of Hispanics as a much needed shot in the arm for their oft-maligned game. "They [Hispanics] have helped the sport. We get more people in the derbies nowadays," admits the anonymous Mississippian. A seller of gamecock nutrients enjoys doing business with Mexicans: "They want to learn more about cocking, they act straight, and they pay in cash."

Over the last few decades, cockfighting has become more democratic and affordable for all cockers, including many working-class Hispanic immigrants, with limited resources and a smaller number of birds, thanks to the "derby" format of competition, in which each cocker puts in a small number of roosters, usually ranging from four to six. A limited number of roosters has opened even the larger tournaments for poorer cockers, who cannot afford to compete up to thirteen roosters, as was customary in many of the old "main" tournaments.[9] Although cockfighting can be an expensive hobby for less successful and financially restrained cockers, the derby has enabled even poorer participants to enter several tournaments over the season.

Many apologists for cockfighting have emphasized the game's gentlemanly nature and its roots in the antebellum South's chivalric planter culture and traditions. Like most romantic interpretations of the region's past, this one is, at best, an exaggeration. Although many antebellum planters, including several notable ones, were enthusiastic cockers, the game reflects more of the antebellum South's brutal, socially ambiguous and ambitious reality than its inflated view of itself. The game is an allegory of the aggressive, go-getter aspects of the region's culture.

Hispanics, African Americans, Asians and other minorities are largely well received in the cockpits. "When cockfighters come together," says Jim Demoruelle, "they do not discuss where somebody is from or how much money they have. They only talk about chickens." Photograph courtesy of Superbass, Wikimedia Commons, under the GNU Free Documentation License.

The game's strict honor code, based on submission to the unwritten rules regulating gambling and social submission to the group, reflects more of the need to maintain a cohesive, solidarity-driven community of deviants than some ancient southern code of honor. In fact, despite its popularity in the South, the customs and traditions surrounding the game are old and universal, shared by cockers from Bali to France, from Elizabethan England to contemporary Louisiana.[10]

For many, cockfighting in the contemporary South seems to represent the tobacco-chewing, beer-drinking, Stars 'n' Bars-waving, devil-may-care, Johnny Reb aspect of southern culture. The game represents the mythical and often imagined Old South of exaggerated honor and violent understanding of masculinity. Despite the participant's ethnicity or status outside the pit, at the Bayou Club and other similar forums, he is a cocker whose worth is mainly measured by his ability to train and fight his chickens, the promptness with which he pays his gambling losses, and his ability and willingness to subjugate himself to the rules of the game and social conventions of the pit.

The relative egalitarianism and fundamentally democratic character of cockfighting has made it an effective avenue for cross-cultural interaction, albeit in a clannish, small, and quasi-secretive way. It might be a fringe sport, and many outsiders have very understandable ethical and moral issues with the sport that more often than not results in the death of its feathered losers; however, cockfighting can show, in its modest and undoubtedly peculiar way, an inclusive, optimistic vision of the region's multicultural future, a way toward a middle ground. In the fury of the pit and the camaraderie of the bleachers, the cockers come together, literally and figuratively, in the violent meritocracy of fighting chickens. As the pile of dead roosters grows in the back room, as Budweiser flows and bills change owners, a peculiar unity emerges among the men gathered in the Bayou Club. Bonded by chickens, steel spurs, betting, and beer, they are a community—strong, inclusive, and very southern.

NOTES

1. Tim Pridgen, *Courage: The Story of Modern Cockfighting* (Little, Brown and Company, 1938), 87.

2. Harold A. Herzog Jr. and Pauline B. Cheek, "Grit and Steel: The Anatomy of Cockfighting," *Southern Exposure* 7.2 (1979): 37. For the game's history in the South, see, for example, B. W. C. Roberts, "Cockfighting: An Early Entertainment in North Carolina," *North Carolina Historical Review* 42.3 (1965): 306–14.

3. Ibid.

4. David Hackett Fischer, *Albion's Seed: Four British Folkways in America* (Oxford University Press, 1991), 552; Guion Griffin Johnson, *Ante-Bellum North Carolina* (University of North Carolina Press, 1937), 181; Roberts, "Cockfighting," 309, 307–11; Steven Del Sesto, "Roles, Rules, and Organization: A Descriptive Account of Cockfighting in Rural Louisiana," *Southern Folklore Quarterly* 39 (March 1975): 1, 6.

5. Clifford Geertz, "Deep Play: Notes on the Balinese Cockfight," *Daedalus* 134.4 (Fall 2005): 58–59 (originally published in 1972).

6. The pits as venues are discussed in Jon Griffin Donlon, "Cajun Cock Pits," *Material Culture* 25.2 (1993): 25–36.

7. Fischer, *Albion's Seed*, 552; Herzog and Cheek, "Grit and Steel," 39; author interviews with Jim Demoruelle, 2004–2006; Harold A. Herzog Jr., "Hackfights and Derbies," *Appalachian Journal* 12.2 (1985): 121–22.

8. Donlon, "Cajun Cock Pits," 25; Herzog, "Hackfights and Derbies," 121.

9. Herzog, "Hackfights and Derbies," 118.

10. For cockfighting's universal character, see, for example, Geertz, "Deep Play"; Roberts, "Cockfighting"; Herzog Jr., "Hackfights and Derbies," 114–26; Don Atyeo, *Blood and Guts: Violence in Sports* (Paddington Press, 1979); Steven L. Del Sesto, "Roles, Rules, and Organization: A Descriptive Account of Cockfighting in Louisiana," *Southern Folklore Quarterly* 39.1 (1975): 1–14.

Selling Which South?

Economic Change in Rural and Small-Town North Carolina in an Era of Globalization,

1940–2007

by Peter A. Coclanis and Louis M. Kyriakoudes

Although most people do not realize it, it has been a long time now since agriculture dominated rural areas in the developed world. Most do know that farmers today constitute but a tiny proportion of the U.S. labor force—about 1.55 percent in 2005—yet few have bothered to ask just what rural folks *are* doing for a living.[1] While the public at large appears to have missed the decoupling of "rural" from "agriculture," this development has shaken several academic disciplines to the core. Entire fields, rural sociology and rural geography, for example, were founded on the assumption that the relationship between rural and agriculture was nearly akin to a mathematical identity, remaining true regardless of the values either of these variables acquired. Even while fewer and fewer farmers were "out standing" in their fields, many so-called agricultural historians merely shifted their attention away from questions relating to agricultural production per se to other questions that had rural dimensions: gender relations, childhood, and rural leisure and consumption patterns, for example.

Not surprisingly, then, once the relationship between rural and agriculture was severed, these disciplines took a nosedive, and it has taken the better part of a generation for them to reemerge, and then only in a much reduced and altered form. Some students of rural agriculture have redefined their terrain by moving away from the study of specific rural locales in the developed world towards the study of global agro-food systems and commodity chains. Some have adopted political economy models, often derived from industrial geography and industrial sociology, and injected class analysis into rural studies, while others still have repositioned themselves as social, women's, or labor historians. A few—Deborah Fink and Steve Striffler, for example—began in a literal rather than figurative sense to study factories in the fields.[2]

Despite the venerable bond between "rural" and "agriculture," manufacturing has played a role in rural America from the colonial period, when domestic manufacturing in rural households constituted the primary type of industrial ac-

National planners and the federal government first became interested in rural manufacturing as a development strategy in the 1930s and 1940s, but the South—or at least individuals and companies operating therein—had by that time been pursuing such a strategy for generations, albeit with mixed success. Spinner in Vivian Cotton Mills, Cherryville, North Carolina, 1908, photographed by Lewis Hine, courtesy of the Collections of the Library of Congress.

tivity. The vast majority of domestic manufactures was intended for home consumption, but by the late eighteenth century, some was destined for markets, and variants on European, rural proto-industrialization schemes existed. In the early national period, rural areas and small towns in New England were the first sites of large-scale, centralized manufacturing activity—the factory system—in North America, and in the antebellum period some large manufactories existed in the rural South.[3]

When the South embarked upon modern industrialization in the 1880s, almost all of the early initiatives focused on rural areas and small towns. Although some larger towns and cities later assumed prominent roles as manufacturing centers in the region, much of the South's industrial activity, particularly in the Carolinas, remained sited in non-metropolitan areas—the rural districts and small towns that lay outside the largest urban areas. When national planners and the federal government first became interested in rural manufacturing as a development strategy in the 1930s and 1940s, the South—or at least individuals and companies operating therein—had already been pursuing such a strategy for generations, albeit with mixed success. Antebellum industrialist William Gregg, whose famed

During the period between 1865 and the Great Depression many important, if less celebrated, industrial operations were established across the rural and small-town South—in textiles, forest products, chemical production, oil, tobacco manufacturing, and mining, among other industries. Bessie Coal Mine employees, Bessie Mine, Alabama, 1910, courtesy of the Collections of the Library of Congress.

Graniteville complex in the Horse Creek Valley of South Carolina was one of the region's first large textile mills, is one example. Between 1865 and the Great Depression, however, many other important, if less celebrated, industrial operations were established across the rural and small-town South. This growth was not just in textile manufacturing but in forest products, tobacco manufacturing, mining, chemical production, and oil, among other industries—hence, the origins of such colorful southern place names as Bauxite, Arkansas, and Nitro, West Virginia.[4]

Following World War II, a significant portion of the South's manufacturing job growth continued to occur in the countryside, easing the problems associated with agriculture's steep decline and allowing the rural South to participate in the region's rising prosperity. This trend towards convergence with the rest of the nation, as measured by per capita income, slowed and then stalled in the 1990s, however, as globalization undermined the South's low-wage manufacturing industries, as technology rendered redundant many low-skill southern jobs, and as other parts of the country enjoyed particularly vigorous growth. Although regional- and state-level income and employment statistics capture these trends in a very broad way, such levels of aggregation obscure the especially serious economic problems in the non-metropolitan South.

Considered a model for southern development policies, North Carolina by many indices has been the South's leading manufacturing state over much of the past half century. Unlike Mississippi, for example, North Carolina has made economically productive choices, investing wisely in education and physical infrastructure. Among the fastest growing southern states, its metropolitan regions are as prosperous as any in the nation, yet despite this prosperity, growth has been uneven. As a result, the state provides an especially apt opportunity to examine the growing divergence between a prosperous urban and an increasingly impoverished rural South. Fifty years ago, North Carolina, the region's industrial pioneer, was the Southeast's largest economy; it is now fourth in the Southeast behind Florida, Georgia, and Virginia. The decline of non-metropolitan areas in North Carolina has been especially precipitous, as rural industry—once the centerpiece of the state's very successful economic development strategy—fades away, rendering the economic future of the Tar Heel State—Research Triangle Park or no Research Triangle Park—uncertain to say the least.

In the five decades after World War II, as the nation's poorest region moved closer to the economic mainstream, the fruits of southern economic development efforts seemed obvious. Manufacturing employment and wages both rose sharply as the region successfully navigated the transition from an isolated, inefficient, and institutionally flawed agricultural economy built upon row crops, tenancy, and sharecropping to a modern manufacturing economy. While southern states still lag behind the rest of the nation in per capita income levels—Mississippi invariably sits at the bottom—the region as a whole has significantly closed the gap with the rest of the nation. World War II and Cold War defense spending provided a strong infusion of investment, while growing population mobility and modernization of the region's agricultural sector broke through the historical isolation of the region's labor force from the national economy. Bolstered by low wages, ample unskilled labor, weak labor organizing, and aggressive state recruiting efforts, industrialization proceeded apace across the region.[5]

The speed at which rural North Carolinians experienced the transition from agriculture to manufacturing was as breathtaking as it was convulsive. On the eve of the American entry into World War II, agriculture remained the most common means by which rural North Carolinians earned their living. In 1940 one-third of non-metropolitan-dwelling whites and one-half of non-metropolitan-dwelling blacks—or 38 percent of all rural working adults—labored in agriculture in some capacity (see Table 1). It was a backward and inefficient agriculture. Even after the economic shocks and restructuring of the Great Depression, New Deal agricultural policies, and World War II mobilization and out-migration, farming in North Carolina in the mid-twentieth century remained largely a tenancy and row-crop affair, beset by limited mechanization and dependent upon inefficient, labor-intensive methods. In 1950 mules still provided the primary means of farm power: there was only one tractor for every four farms that year, and mules outnumbered tractors four to one. Statewide, nearly 40 percent of all North Carolina farmers

Table 1. Ten Leading Industries by Percent Employed in Metropolitan and Non-metropolitan North Carolina, 1940–2000.

Ten Leading Industries, by Employment, Metro NC, 1940		Ten Leading Industries, by Employment, Non-Metro NC, 1940	
Textiles, apparel, carpet, and knitting mills	16.3	Agriculture	38.4
Private households	10.1	Textiles, apparel, carpet, and knitting mills	16.0
Agriculture	7.6	Construction	5.8
Construction	5.9	Private households	5.6
Tobacco manufactures	5.2	Educational services	3.2
Educational services	4.1	Sawmills, planing mills, and mill work	2.5
Hospitals	2.7	Furniture and fixtures	1.9
Food stores, except dairy	2.5	Food stores, except dairy	1.8
Misc wholesale trade	2.5	Not classifiable	1.4
Local public administration	2.3	Federal public administration	1.1
Sum	**59.2**	**Sum**	**77.7**

Ten Leading Industries, by Employment, Metro NC, 1960		Ten Leading Industries, by Employment, Non-metro NC, 1960	
Textiles, apparel, carpet, and knitting mills	9.7	Textiles, apparel, carpet, and knitting mills	17.9
Construction	7.0	Agriculture	15.8
Educational services	6.6	Federal public administration	7.2
Private households	4.9	Construction	6.3
Tobacco manufactures	4.8	Educational services	4.9
Agriculture	3.6	Private households	4.6
Hospitals	3.0	Furniture and fixtures	2.9
Electrical machinery, equipment, and supplies	2.9	Food stores, except dairy	2.3
Food stores, except dairy	2.4	Sawmills, planing mills, and mill work	2.0
Insurance	2.4	Hospitals	1.6
Sum	**47.3**	**Sum**	**65.5**

Ten Leading Industries, by Employment, Metro, NC, 1980		Ten Leading Industries, by Employment, Non-Metro NC, 1980	
Textiles, apparel, carpet, and knitting mills	10.3	Textiles, apparel, carpet, and knitting mills	16.6
Educational services	8.6	Educational services	8.0
Federal public administration	7.9	Construction	6.8
Construction	5.2	Agriculture	5.6
Hospitals	4.2	Federal public administration	4.2
Eating and drinking places	3.5	Furniture and fixtures	3.8
Furniture and fixtures	3.0	Hospitals	3.2
Electrical machinery, equipment, and supplies	2.3	Eating and drinking places	2.9
Medical and other health services, except hospitals	2.2	Medical and other health services, except hospitals	2.5
Food stores, except dairy	2.2	Food stores, except dairy	2.4
Sum	**49.4**	**Sum**	**56.0**

Ten Leading Industries, by Employment, Metro NC, 2000		Ten Leading Industries, by Employment, Non-Metro, NC, 2000	
Educational services	9.5	Construction	9.6
Construction	7.4	Textiles, apparel, carpet, and knitting mills	9.0
Misc business services	6.1	Educational services	8.3
Eating and drinking places	4.4	Medical and other health services,	
Banking and credit	4.3	except hospitals	5.4
Medical and other health services,		Hospitals	4.7
except hospitals	3.8	Agriculture	4.0
Hospitals	3.3	Eating and drinking places	3.9
Textiles, apparel, carpet, and knitting mills	3.2	Federal public administration	3.3
Insurance	2.3	Food stores, except dairy	2.8
Printing, publishing, and allied industries	2.0	Local public administration	2.3
Sum	46.3	Sum	53.3

Note: Frequencies calculated from employed individuals, age 16+

Source: Steven Ruggles, Matthew Sobek, Trent Alexander, Catherine A. Fitch, Ronald Goeken, Patricia Kelly Hall, Miriam King, and Chad Ronnander, *Integrated Public Use Microdata Series: Version 3.0* [Machine-readable database], MN: Minnesota Population Center [producer and distributor], 2004, http://www.ipums.org.

continued to operate under some form of tenant or sharecropping arrangement, with the figure rising sharply in the tobacco and cotton belts.[6]

The economic transformation of rural North Carolina after about 1950, however, was nothing less than remarkable. Agriculture underwent a profound reorganization as farmers finally began to mechanize cotton cultivation in the 1950s and then tobacco growing in the 1960s. Farmers diversified, planting soybeans or turning to new activities such as the production of poultry and hogs. Mechanical cotton harvesting and bulk curing of tobacco sharply increased labor productivity while reducing the need for farm labor. The demand for a permanent, year-round agricultural labor pool plummeted, sustaining a wholesale exodus from traditional agricultural employment even as many rural people remained in the countryside. By 2000 agriculture, the leading occupation of rural North Carolinians fifty years earlier, had slipped to sixth place and employed only 4 percent of working adults. As late as 1970 at least one-fifth of the workers in thirty-two of North Carolina's one hundred counties were employed in agriculture. In 2000 no county could make that claim. By then, only thirteen North Carolina counties had as many as one in ten workers employed in agriculture, and only three counties had as many as one in seven workers so employed. The transformation of rural and small-town North Carolina into a manufacturing region was nearly complete.[7]

Long-term changes in how rural elites envisioned the economic future of their communities aided this shift to industry in the southern countryside. The prominent merchants and landowners that comprised the South's rural and small-town elite turned to industrialization to bolster the economic future of their localities. After World War II they supported "smokestack-chasing" economic development policies, which subsidized the relocation and infrastructure costs of manufacturers willing to move in order to avail themselves of an underemployed, rural labor force. Manufacturers, for their part, found a rural South that was now well-provided with physical infrastructure in the form of good roads and a widely distributed electric power grid, and endowed with a low-cost, nonunionized, and tractable labor supply.[8]

While furniture manufacturing flourished in western North Carolina and light assembly and appliance manufacturing took important root in the east, rural North Carolina's industrialization nevertheless rested upon a narrow and fragile foundation of textile and apparel manufacturing. Post World War II southern industrialization is generally thought of as a diverse process, part of what historian Charles Roland dubbed "the improbable era" when a broad array of northern manufacturers headed south to escape unions and their high wages. The very term "smokestack-chasing" implies the pursuit of heavy, or at least complex, industry, and there have been subregional industrial concentrations in the state. Yet, textile and apparel manufacturing have consistently been the single largest employer of rural and small-town North Carolinians (see Table 1). In 1960 nearly one-fifth of rural North Carolinians worked in either textile or apparel manufacturing. Only in the 1990s, with the industry ravaged by foreign competition, did layoffs and plant closings move it to second place. Even then, the industry still employed nearly one in ten rural workers in 2000. As a mature industry, textile and apparel manufacturing persisted in providing the foundation for North Carolina's extensive rural industrialization, augmented by a variety of low-wage, unskilled and semi-skilled manufacturing.[9]

The persistence of textiles in rural North Carolina also suggests a broader national process in which manufacturing generally, and low-skilled manufacturing in particular, worked its way down the urban hierarchy, fleeing large cities and settling in small towns and rural communities. Nationally, non-metropolitan regions are now more dependent upon manufacturing employment than metropolitan regions, where services and other diverse activities now predominate. In North Carolina, even as textile employment persisted in the countryside, it nearly evaporated in the state's cities, so much so that the current collapse in textiles employment is largely a rural and small-town problem.[10]

The decline of textiles employment has particularly affected the state's rural black workers, who moved from agriculture into the industry in substantial numbers in the 1960s and 1970s—a movement that can be best characterized as a

Figure 1. North Carolina County Economic Classifications

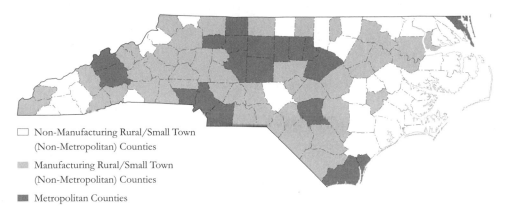

☐ Non-Manufacturing Rural/Small Town
   (Non-Metropolitan) Counties

▨ Manufacturing Rural/Small Town
   (Non-Metropolitan) Counties

■ Metropolitan Counties

Source: U.S. Department of Agriculture Economic Research Service.

move from sharecropping to the shop floor. Until the 1960s, few African Americans, rural or urban, worked in textile manufacturing. In 1960, for example, only 3 percent of rural African Americans worked in the industry. By 1970, however, 21 percent of black non-metropolitan workers labored in textiles; the figure for non-metropolitan whites stood at only 16 percent. Since then, the textile industry has continued to play a relatively larger role in black non-metropolitan employment compared to white.[11]

Urban and rural North Carolina are now headed in two economic directions. The state's cities are home to a diversified and dynamic metropolitan economy. Charlotte's banking and finance industry and heavy manufacturing have made that city the economic dynamo of the larger bi-state Carolinas region. The technology and pharmaceutical industries in the "Triangle"—Raleigh, Durham, and Chapel Hill—and nearby Research Triangle Park have made this metropolitan region an international center for research and development. Even the Greensboro, High Point, and Winston-Salem "Triad" has maintained strong growth, despite its historical investment in ailing textile and furniture industries. North Carolina's metropolitan counties have averaged 10 percent population growth every five years since the 1970s.

Non-metropolitan North Carolina, however, is seeing its industrial base dwindle, with few viable replacements on the horizon. By 1979 forty-seven of the state's one hundred counties were both rural and dependent upon manufacturing for at least 30 percent of gross county income (see Figure 1). Along with neighboring Tennessee and South Carolina, North Carolina led the nation in its high level of rural industrialization (see Table 2). As late as 2000 textile manufacturing stood out as the single largest employment opportunity. Average five-year population growth in those rural counties most heavily invested in manufacturing stood at only 6 percent. Rural North Carolina continues to be heavily invested in man-

Table 2. Top Ten States, by Percent of Non-Metropolitan Manufacturing Dependent Counties, 1979

State	Non-Metro Mfg Counties	% of All Counties
South Carolina	27	58.7
Tennessee	47	49.5
North Carolina	47	47.0
Alabama	30	44.8
Ohio	36	40.9
Georgia	65	40.9
Indiana	35	38.0
Mississippi	30	36.6
Pennsylvania	22	32.8
Virginia	30	30.6

Source: Calculated from County Typology Codes—1979 & 1986 using the 1974 non-metro definition, Economic Research Service, United States Department of Agriculture, http://www.ers.usda.gov/Data/TypologyCodes/.
Note: The following states with fewer than 20 counties were excluded from analysis: Delaware (3), Maine (16), and New Hampshire (10)

ufacturing: 21 percent of working non-metropolitan North Carolinians earned their living in manufacturing industries, while only 15 percent of metropolitan North Carolinians did so.[12]

The shift from agriculture to manufacturing played a leading role in the overall improvement in North Carolina's and the South's per capita income growth as workers moved out of low-wage sharecropping and tenancy arrangements and into higher-wage manufacturing jobs. In 1930 North Carolina's per capita income stood at just 47 percent of the national average, three percentage points below the figure for the entire Southeast. Postwar prosperity saw North Carolina's per capita income rise sharply, peaking in 1997 at 93 percent of the national average before falling to its current level of 89 percent, a figure that still remains below the southeastern average.[13]

The course of North Carolina's per capita income performance, however, has been mixed, especially considering its robust rate of economic and population expansion. The state's heavy investment in labor-intensive, low-margin industries such as textiles has meant that low wages have undermined the state's per capita performance, even in the context of the South, and incomes have been particularly sensitive to the business cycle. From 1954 to 1986, for example, the state's per capita income lagged behind that of the Southeast for the entire time, sometimes alarmingly so for a state considered to have enjoyed robust growth. The recession- and inflation-prone 1970s saw the greatest lag in North Carolina in-

Figure 2. Per Capita Income as a Percent of the National Average, 1929–2004: North Carolina and the Southeast

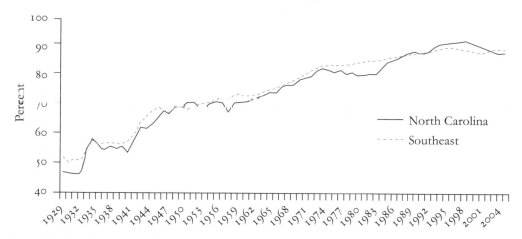

Source: Regional Economic Information System, Bureau of Economic Analysis, Table SA1-3 — Per capita personal income.

comes. While southeastern incomes rose two percentage points in the late 1970s to 86 percent of the national average, North Carolina incomes fell two points. The recession of 2001 once again saw the state's per capita income dip sharply below that of the region (see Figure 2).

A steady erosion in the rural manufacturing employment base underlies the relative drop in per capita income. To be sure, manufacturing employment constitutes an ever smaller share of total employment in the nation as a whole. But nonmetropolitan North Carolina has seen its employment base particularly heavily ravaged in the last half decade as textiles and other light-assembly operations have experienced profound technological change and faced stiff foreign competition. From 2001 to 2003 the rate of announced layoffs in manufacturing in rural counties far outpaced those in metropolitan counties; in 2003, for example, the rate of manufacturing layoffs was two and a half times greater in the countryside.[14]

Losses in textiles have been most severe. An industry that employed over 250,000 North Carolinians in the 1970s has seen job losses swell to 160,000 from 1994 to 2004 alone. Textile industry advocates blame low-cost Asian imports, the North American Free Trade Agreement (NAFTA), the World Trade Organization, and the devaluation of Asian currencies after the 1997 East Asian financial crisis. The John Birch Society has recently jumped on the bandwagon as well, mounting a "Stop the FTAA" (Free Trade Area of the Americas) and "Stop CAFTA" (Central American Free Trade Area) billboard campaign along Interstate-85 in the Carolinas.[15]

The reality behind the decline of North Carolina's textile industry is more complex, however. Textile manufacturing has been a global industry for a long time.

During our current post-World War II phase of economic globalization, it has become increasingly apparent that the American South has been a low-wage region only in comparison to the high-wage North and West. Internationally, the South has long been uncompetitive in the labor-intensive, low-skilled elements of the textile industry and other simple manufactures that have come to dominate rural North Carolina. For virtually the entire twentieth century, the southern textile industry prospered behind high transport costs, tariff barriers, and protectionist import quotas that sharply curtailed the importation of cotton and manufactured fiber textile products even as the United States sought to foster an international free-trade system. In the 1950s the textile industry feared Japanese competition and supported the negotiation of "Voluntary Export Restraints"; in the 1960s the United States negotiated the Long Term Agreement on Cotton Textiles, and in the 1970s the Multifiber Agreement extended those terms to manufactured fibers.[16]

The phase-out of textile quotas in 2005 has increasingly opened the U.S. textile industry to the full brunt of foreign competition. Industry leaders now expect most production to move to China and other parts of Asia, leaving behind a token industry focused on custom-designed, specialty products requiring rapid turnaround. Predictions for North Carolina's total textile employment hover at around forty thousand, and those estimates may be too optimistic. The intensity of global competition in textiles and apparel is suggested by a June 2007 announcement by Winston-Salem-based Hanesbrands Inc., manufacturer of Hanes underwear, L'Eggs pantyhose, and the Wonderbra. The firm announced an 11 percent reduction in its workforce—laying off 5,700 workers—and the closing of nine sewing and assembly plants. Only a fraction of the layoffs are in North Carolina. The vast preponderance of job losses and shuttered manufacturing sites are in Mexico and the Dominican Republic, an indication that global competitive pressures affect much more that the United States.[17]

In many respects rural North Carolina is poorly equipped to recover lost ground. Social pathologies popularly associated with urban poverty are, in fact, more prevalent in the state's rural manufacturing counties (see Table 3). Teenage girls in these counties are more likely to become pregnant, while children in these counties are more likely to have asthma, a disease closely associated with poverty. Rural manufacturing counties have higher rates of food-stamp use and higher overall rates of poverty among children and the elderly. Rural manufacturing counties in eastern North Carolina generally fare worse on all measures of poverty, health, and well-being than their counterparts in the piedmont or mountains.

Educational levels, not surprisingly, lag in the countryside. Rural schools across the state draw upon a poorer tax base and are under-funded compared to their urban counterparts. Weak economic incentives for young rural people to invest in education further compound the problem of poor schools. With jobs requiring few formal skills beckoning in local mills, young people contemplating comple-

Table 3. Measures of Social Welfare: Metropolitan and Non-metropolitan North Carolina, 2000

County Type	Pregnancies, Women, Ages, 15–19 (per 1000)	Asthma Rate, Ages 0–14, (per 100,000)	Food stamp recipients (%)	Population in poverty (%)
Non-Metro, Non-Mfg. Dependent Counties	61.5	235	8.0	15.1
Non-Metro, Mfg. Dependent Counties	69.3	241	8.8	13.7
Metro Counties	56.1	175	6.4	10.4

Source: N.C. Department of Health and Human Services, State Center for Health Statistics; U.S. Census Bureau, 2000.

tion of high school or additional education at a community college or university have historically found the opportunity costs too high. Now that those jobs no longer call, rural North Carolinians find themselves trapped in a cycle of poor education and limited opportunities. It is, therefore, not surprising that North Carolina's rural manufacturing counties have the lowest rate of residents with college degrees (14 v. 30 percent for metropolitan counties) and the highest portion of workers with less than a high school diploma (28 v. 17 percent for metropolitan counties). Compared to their urban counterparts, rural students perform worse on standardized examinations such as the SAT.[18]

Education poses the classic dilemma of economic development efforts: is it geared towards people or places? Improvements in education allow rural young people to seek their fortunes in metropolitan areas, particularly those who continue their educations after high school. For those remaining in a rural county, additional education may train them for jobs that simply do not exist in their locality. For example, a frustrated job-seeker who had gone through a worker-retraining program in biotechnology in rural eastern North Carolina complained to the Raleigh *News and Observer*: "What good has this done for a displaced worker in his mid-40s? Two temp jobs later and after much effort, I gave up looking for a permanent job in biotech." The North Carolina biotechnology campus, a high-technology research facility under construction in the former textile town of Kannapolis, will not absorb the former mill workers displaced by the collapse of the textile manufacturer Pillowtex, which was located at the site. Officials with the campus note that "residents still call the research campus offices wanting to know where the new Pillowtex plant will be." A study of the 4,800 workers laid off with the collapse of Pillowtex found that after three years, only 60 percent reported wages of any kind, and of those reporting wages, half earned less than five thousand dollars.[19]

World War II and Cold War defense spending provided a strong infusion of investment, while growing population mobility and modernization of the region's agricultural sector jolted the region's labor force out of its historical isolation from the national economy. Bolstered by low wages, ample unskilled labor, weak labor organizing, and aggressive state recruiting efforts, industrialization proceeded apace across the region. The war production effort at Vultee Aircraft Company, Nashville, Tennessee, 1942, photographed by Jack Delano, courtesy of the Collections of the Library of Congress.

With educational standards constantly rising, a high school diploma and willingness to work are no longer a guarantee of successful employment. Policy makers now talk of the problems of the "muddled middle," the substantial number of average students who successfully complete high school but are unprepared or unwilling to attend college.[20] In the past, North Carolina's pattern of strong nonmetropolitan industrial employment offered opportunities for this group. What the state will do with its rural students who are merely "average" is a question that still remains open.

Some contemporary observers now see North Carolina's current troubles in light of economic development strategies bent on selling the state as a low-wage haven. It is, as the Greensboro *News and Record* recently editorialized, a case of "what goes around, comes around." It is a widely held notion that North Carolina recruited textiles and many of its other industries simply "because employees here would work for less money." In fact, during its formative period, the textile industry grew and developed largely under the leadership of *local* entrepreneurial talent, fuelled by *local* capital investments. Certainly lower wages and an environment less accommodating to organized labor have attracted investment from the North, but these aren't the only factors. Other southern states such as Mississippi and Arkansas have decidedly lower wages and are equally hostile to organized labor but have not approached North Carolina's robust levels of wage and population growth.[21]

In the last half century North Carolina has expended great energies on recruiting manufacturers from the North and overseas. In the 1950s Governor Luther Hodges, who presided over the founding of the Research Triangle Park and was dubbed the state's "first salesman," broke new ground by leading a trade delegation to Europe to promote North Carolina. His successor in the executive mansion, Terry Sanford, also developed a reputation as a strong recruiter of indus-

North Carolina's traditional reliance on textile manufacturing no longer offers a solution to the problems of rural and small-town economic development. Photograph by Louis M. Kyriakoudes.

try, running trips to the industrial Midwest to dangle tax abatements and other inducements before manufacturers unhappy with northern wages and unions. James B. Hunt devoted much energy in his four terms as governor to business recruitment as well. Hunt, in particular, sought to spread economic development to the rural regions of the state through a policy called "balanced growth." Partly driven by basic political considerations in a state dominated by rural and small-town interests, it also reflected a deep sensitivity to the need to locate investment across the state.[22]

The dilemmas of development in rural North Carolina will not yield themselves to easy economic "magic bullets." There is no one single class of economic activity to replace the textile and labor-intensive manufactures that eased the state's rural areas out of agriculture. Contemporary proposals for spurring employment and economic growth are many. John Kasarda, a professor at the University of North Carolina's Kenan School of Business and long-time student of North Carolina's economic development, has called for making the state's poorest regions—particularly in the east—havens for retirees. Make small-town North Carolina a "mecca for people with money" seeking a higher quality of life, he proposes. In some ways, this process is already underway. North Carolina's extensive eastern inland waterways (the "Inner Banks") along the Pamlico and Albemarle Sounds are experiencing rapid development as developers shift away from the crowded Atlantic coast. The North Carolina Budget and Tax Center, a progressive public policy think tank, calls for renewed workforce training and improved social insurance policies for working families to "make work pay." Groups such as FORENC (Foundation of Renewal for Eastern North Carolina) have emphasized the longstanding importance—and future possibilities—of East Carolina University and the region's five military bases, while the Southern Growth Policies Board advocates regional development efforts that coordinate state, private, and local grassroots interests.[23]

Leo Tolstoy began *Anna Karenina* by observing that "All happy families resemble one another, but each unhappy family is unhappy in its own way." The situation facing rural North Carolina is similar. Metropolitan North Carolina has done well by itself. Bolstered by Charlotte's banking and finance industries, the Triangle's research and university complex, and the Triad's diversified manufacturing base, these urban regions have prospered. Non-metropolitan North Carolina, however, faces a difficult future. Each of the state's eighty-one non-metropolitan counties is "unhappy in its own way." The inhabitants of these counties deserve more, however, than "a one-way Greyhound ticket and a ham sandwich," as some cynics suggest.[24] Finding the right development strategies — selling this South, as it were — is North Carolina's greatest challenge.

NOTES

In this paper we use BEA (Bureau of Economic Analysis) and IPUMS (Integrated Public Use Microdata Series) data in a variety of ways to demonstrate the complex economic challenges faced by the rural South.

1. U.S. Census Bureau, *The 2007 Statistical Abstract: The National Data Book*, http://www.census.gov/compendia/statab/. The percentage figure was calculated from data in Table No. 606, Employment, by Industry: 2000–2005.

2. See Philip McMichael, ed., *The Global Restructuring of Agro-Food Systems* (Cornell University Press, 1994); David Goodman, "World-Scale Processes and Agro-Food Systems: Critique and Research Needs," *Review of International Political Economy* 4 (Winter 1997): 663–87. For more about political economy models, see Terry Marsden, Richard Munton, Neil Ward, and Sarah Whatmore, "Agricultural Geography and the Political Economy Approach: A Review," *Economic Geography* 72 (October 1996): 361–75; Brian Page, "Across the Great Divide: Agriculture and Industrial Geography," *Economic Geography* 72 (October 1996): 376–97; Philip McMichael, "Rethinking Globalization: The Agrarian Question Revisited," *Review of International Political Economy* 4 (Winter 1997): 630–62; Peter A. Coclanis, "From the History of Agriculture to the History of Food Systems," *Historical Methods* 38 (Winter 2005): 5–13; Deborah Fink, *Cutting into the Meatpacking Line: Workers and Change in the Rural Midwest* (University of North Carolina Press, 1998); Steve Striffler, *Chicken: The Dangerous Transformation of America's Favorite Food* (Yale University Press, 2005).

3. For the classic accounts of early American domestic manufacturing, see Rolla M. Tryon, *Household Manufactures in the United States, 1640–1860: A Study in Industrial History* (University of Chicago Press, 1917); Victor S. Clark, *History of Manufactures in the United States*, 3 vols. (1929; rprt. Peter Smith, 1949), vol. 1 esp. On the putting-out system in early America, see, for example, Thomas Dublin, "Women and Outwork in a Nineteenth-Century New England Town: Fitzwilliam, New Hampshire, 1830–1850," in *The Countryside in the Age of Capitalist Transformation: Essays in the Social History of Rural America*, ed. Steve Hahn and Jonathan Prude (University of North Carolina Press, 1985), 51–69; and Christopher Clark, *The Roots of Rural Capitalism: Western Massachusetts, 1780–1860* (Cornell University Press, 1990). On the factory system in the South, see, for example, Ernest M. Lander, *The Textile Industry of Antebellum South Carolina* (Louisiana State University Press, 1969); Bess Beatty, *Alamance: The Holt Family and Industrialization in a North Carolina County, 1837–1900* (University of North Carolina Press, 1999); Tom Downey, *Planting a Capitalist South: Masters, Merchants, and Manufacturers in the Southern Interior, 1790–1860* (Louisiana State University Press, 2006).

4. David L. Carlton, *Mill and Town in South Carolina, 1880–1920* (Louisiana State University Press, 1982). Philip Scranton, ed., *The Second Wave: Southern Industrialization from the 1940s to the 1970s* (University of Georgia Press, 2001); Glenn E. McLaughlin and Stefan Robock, *Why Industry Moves*

South: A Study of Factors Influencing the Recent Location of Manufacturing Plants in the South, Report No. 3 (Washington, D.C.: Committee of the South, National Planning Commission, 1949); Dennis Roth, "Thinking about Rural Manufacturing: A Brief History," *Rural America* 15 (January 2000): 12–19.

5. Gavin Wright, *Old South, New South: Revolutions in the Southern Economy Since the Civil War* (Basic Books, 1986); James C. Cobb, *The Selling of the South: The Southern Crusade for Industrial Development, 1936–1980*, 2d ed. (University of Illinois Press, 1993); David L. Carlton, "The American South and the U.S. Defense Economy: A Historical View," in David L. Carlton and Peter A. Coclanis, *The South, the Nation, and the World: Perspectives on Southern Economic Development* (University of Virginia Press, 2003), 151–62; Marko Maunula, "Guten Tag, Y'All. The Arrival of Foreign Corporations in the South Carolina Piedmont, 1950–1990" (Ph.D. dissertation, University of North Carolina-Chapel Hill, 2004).

6. U.S. Census Bureau, *Statistical Abstract of the United States: 1954* (Washington, D.C.: Government Printing Office, 1954), 638, 657, 701.

7. John Fraser Hart and Ennis L. Chestang, "Trouble in Tobaccoland," *The Geographical Review* 86.4 (October 1996): 550–72.

8. David L. Carlton, "Smokestack-Chasing and Its Discontents: Southern Development Strategy in the Twentieth Century," in *The American South in the Twentieth Century*, ed. Craig S. Pascoe, Karen Trahan Lathem, and Andy Ambrose (University of Georgia Press, 2005), 106–26.

9. Charles P. Roland, *The Improbable Era: The South since World War II* (University Press of Kentucky, 1976).

10. Alexander C. Vias and Peter B. Nelson, "Changing Livelihoods in Rural America," in *Population Change and Rural Society*, ed. William A. Kandel and David L. Brown (Springer, 2006), 85–87.

11. Employment distributions calculated from census samples. See Steven Ruggles, Matthew Sobek, Trent Alexander, Catherine A. Fitch, Ronald Goeken, Patricia Kelly Hall, Miriam King, and Chad Ronnander. Integrated Public Use Microdata Series: Version 3.0 [Machine-readable database], Minnesota Population Center [producer and distributor], 2004, http://www.ipums.org

12. Textiles here include spinning, weaving, knitting, and carpet operations. Manufacturing employment calculated from data in Calvin Beale, *ERS/USDA Briefing Room - Measuring Rurality: Rural-Urban Continuum Codes*, http://www.ers.usda.gov/Briefing/Rurality/RuralUrbCon/, accessed 18 October 2005.

13. Leonard F. Wheat and William H. Crown, *State per-capita income change since 1950: Sharecropping's Collapse and Other Causes of Convergence*, Contributions in Economics and Economic History series, No. 167 (Greenwood Press, 1995).

14. N.C. Rural Economic Development Center, Inc., http://www.ncruralcenter.org/databank/, accessed 23 July 2007.

15. Billboards observed by Kyriakoudes along I-85 between Anderson S.C. and Charlotte N.C., December, 2005. The Birch Society maintains the following websites: http://www.stoptheftaa.org/ and http://www.stopcafta.org.

16. David L. Carlton and Peter A. Coclanis, "Southern Textiles in Global Context," in *Global Perspectives on Industrial Transformation in the American South*, ed. Susanna Delfino and Michele Gillespie (University of Missouri Press, 2005), 151–74; Kala Krishna, *Rags and Riches: Implementing Apparel Quotas under the Multi-Fibre Arrangement* (University of Michigan Press, 1998), 3–4.

17. David Ranii, "Another Big Loss for N.C. Textiles," Raleigh *News and Observer*, 28 June 2007; Donald W. Patterson, "Textile Job Bleeding May Get Worse; North Carolina's Industry Could Lose Anywhere from 10,000 to 20,000 Jobs This Year, Economists Say," Greensboro *News and Record*, 21 February 2005, A1.

18. Linda Flowers, *Throwed Away: Failures of Progress in Eastern North Carolina* (University of Tennessee Press, 1990), 90–108. For another look at the problems affecting such parts of the Carolinas, see Peter A. Coclanis, "Down Highway 52: Globalization, Higher Education, and the Economic Future of the American South," *The Journal of the Historical Society* 5 (Fall 2005): 331–45.

19. Stephen Ashby, Mount Olive, N.C., Letter to the Editor, Raleigh *News and Observer*, 25 June 2007; Tim Simmons, "Biotech Campus Met With Doubt," Raleigh *News and Observer*, 18 June 2007.

20. MDC, Inc., *State of the South 2004: Fifty Years after Brown v. Board of Education* (MDC, Inc., 2004), 24.

21. Patterson, "Textile Job Bleeding May Get Worse"; David L. Carlton and Peter A. Coclanis, "Capital Mobilization and Southern Industry, 1880–1905: The Case of the Carolina Piedmont," *The Journal of Economic History* 49 (March 1989): 73–94.

22. "Gov. Hodges to Sell Carolina in Europe," *New York Times*, 25 October 1959; Memory F. Mitchell, *Addresses and Public Papers of James Baxter Hunt, Jr., Governor of North Carolina*, 3 vols. (North Carolina Division of Archives and History, Department of Cultural Resources, 1982–2000), vol. I, xxiv.

23. John D. Kasarda, "Make a Mecca for People with Money," Raleigh *News and Observer*, 9 April 2006, http://www.newsobserver.com/164/story/426735.html; John Quinterno, *North Carolina's Unfinished Transformation: Connecting Working Families to the State's Newfound Prosperity* (Raleigh, N.C.: Budget and Tax Center, 2006); FoRENC website, http://www.forenc.com; Jim Clinton, et al., *The New Architecture of Rural Prosperity: The 2005 Report on the Future of the South* (Southern Growth Policies Board, 2005).

24. Many rural counties in eastern North Carolina have, in fact, been losing population since 2000. See the Raleigh *News and Observer*, 22 March 2007, 1A.

The Institute and the Factory
Business Leadership and Change in the Global South

by John Russell

This essay was first presented in March 2006 as a talk on corporate leadership at the "Navigating the Global American South" conference, organized by the Center for Global Initiatives and the Center for the Study of the American South at the University of North Carolina at Chapel Hill.

usiness leaders and change has been an enduring theme since the proclaimed origin of the New South, now well over a century ago. Perhaps the global part is new, though the folks who work at Coca-Cola or Reynolds Tobacco would surely take issue with that. I am especially happy to take up this theme today because I think right now there's a disconnect between business leadership and social change precisely when a new generation of business leaders can have something useful to say.

On a personal note, in every business I've joined, I've been the "Southern Guy." I don't speak very often now in that role, since the world has thankfully changed and the Southern Guy is not a curiosity any more. But I was taken back to another time by yesterday's luncheon speaker, my friend, Shannon Ravenel, formerly Editor-in-Chief of Algonquin Books. In the 1970s we worked together in publishing at Houghton Mifflin Co. There I really was the Southern Guy in the New York office, and she was the Southern Lady in the Boston office. But make no mistake, that's the only equivalence we shared. At Houghton Mifflin Shannon Ravenel rightfully was a legend, and I got coffee.

As the Southern Guy in the New York office, I got sent on specific assignments. One of them was to entertain Pat Conroy when he came to town. That usually involved a bar or two. I was confident in my role as the Southern Guy until Pat took me aside one day.

"Russell," he said, "you aren't very much of a southerner."

"What are you talking about?" I said.

"You don't drink enough, your accent's no good, they say you went to school up here, and you wear a suit all the time. That's why you're not a very good *southerner*."

I slammed down my beer. "Pat, I take offense at that. I drink a lot."

From southern roots to one of the most recognized global brands, the Coca-Cola Company has successfully embodied the concept of "The Institute" for a century through constant innovation. Advertisement from the 1930s, courtesy of the Coca-Cola Company.

I did try to be a better Southern Guy after Pat called me out. I don't know whether I really succeeded or not.

Today, however, the Southern Guy—or Southern Lady—hardly attracts attention, standing shoulder-to-shoulder with the Chinese, French, Nigerian, or Colombian colleagues. Clearly, work has changed and made more social change happen. The question I would like to address here is, specifically, how business leaders can contribute to the larger conversation about social change spurred by a global economy. Business leaders in the global economy today can bring special gifts to an environment where change and more change has occurred and will occur—change that affects the lives of people and institutions and regions, how we live, how we make our living, how we raise our children, how we can face the future confidently.

First I will talk about ideas that I call the "Institute" and the "Factory," together a model of thinking that I believe useful in explaining how successful business leaders progress in a changing global business environment. I will talk about companion concepts of "Brave New World" and "Faster Better Cheaper," shorthand for useful ways of organizing economic activity to succeed in a world of customers who are also competitors, friends who act like opponents, and rivals who become partners.

Secondly, I will talk about the university and its promise as an organizing principle and creative haven in this often bewildering landscape. This is a theme that I have heard over the last two days—and a good one.

The final part of my talk is titled "My Dinner with Sergei." I was tempted to make that the title of the entire speech, with apologies to the once popular movie, but I thought it would date me. This part of the speech is really about new global communities and how we can understand them by borrowing from our regional roots.

One caveat: I am not a scholar or a scientist. I am a businessman trained as a lawyer, and I sometimes write books. But I profess no scholarly credentials. To compound the confusion, I do work with biostatisticians a lot. Biostatistics is mainly what my company does.

INVENT A BUSINESS, INVENT AN INDUSTRY

The Institute and the Factory are complementary modes of thinking about change and acting within it. To illustrate, I'll start with a concrete example, the founding of my company, Quintiles Transnational Corp.

Dennis Gillings, who was a professor in the School of Public Health at the University of North Carolina at Chapel Hill, founded Quintiles twenty-five years ago. In doing so, he also invented an industry. Dr. Gillings had the idea that pharmaceutical companies could outsource the performance of clinical trials to experts who could conduct them globally and analyze the results independently. He thus made a business out of what pharmaceutical companies called overhead.

The School of Public Health wisely gave him a trailer in their parking lot to work, and he employed graduate students. The business immediately became global. There was no way for it not to be. Today the company has over seventeen thousand employees, two billion dollars in revenue, and it operates in fifty-one countries. But amidst this success lies the possibility the rapid change that gave us birth could destroy our business. Changes in the way the pharmaceutical industry works could make our current practices obsolete. Also, the pharmaceutical industry itself, now dominated by large companies, might disaggregate—so our customers may change. Additionally, other competitors such as large global consultancies and large data companies have decided to do what we do, so we have unforeseen new competitors who are large and formidable. For our part, we may decide that our business mix needs to radically change, and so we transform our current services into entirely different lines.

So you see there is nothing but change every day in what we do. I work in an industry that someone thought up twenty-five years ago, founded by a professor who invented a two-billion-dollar business while working in a trailer. And all of it could go away tomorrow. Success in this arena requires harnessing constant change. It requires living sometimes in the Institute and sometimes in the Factory.

When you form a business, you usually have a thought about how to make something new or make something that already exists better. The thinking that produces these insights I call the Institute. The Institute is not a building or a faculty or even a formal organization so much as a habit of mind. Leading businesses have it, however, and constantly use it to innovate and improve.

I think one reason for this is that business leaders understand that the old saying "if it ain't broke, don't fix it" could not be more wrong. It is fundamentally 180 degrees backwards. In the current environment, once you think of a good idea and put it into action, you have to assume that someone at some point is going to do it as well or better than you. So at the very moment you do something good, you have to start thinking about doing something else good and understand the obsolescence of your own success. Therein lies the necessity of the Institute.

In order to make ideas into action, you need to have a Factory. By that I don't mean a building of bricks and mortar, although sometimes that is there. I mean a habit of mind that is organizational, process driven, attracts and retains talented people, identifies its customers and sells to them with passion, and produces a better good or service with high and consistent quality wherever it is sold or delivered. Again, once you establish a Factory, then you have to assume that someone will immediately copy it and try to do what you are doing better, so your ability to succeed is often founded on changing and improving everything all the time, even when it seems you don't have to.

Together, however, the Institute and the Factory nurtured properly create a model that gives you a chance to master change rather than have change master you. Investors in the private equity markets have a shorthand for discussing the Institute and the Factory when they are talking about the value of businesses. Businesses driven by the Institute they call "Brave New World." Businesses driven by the Factory they call "Faster Better Cheaper." Both can be attractive. Ultimately, each needs the other concept to thrive.

In my business, we often try to sort out ideas along those lines. Often we say a good idea is a Brave New World thing, or a cleaner process is a Faster Better Cheaper thing. Since living in constant change is startling and contrary to what makes most human beings happy, we also try to reach for comforting analogies while we rearrange the cupboard. The Brave New World approach suggests images of the Starship Enterprise, which we beam across the company periodically at the launch of a new idea. The good Factory creates environments that keep adults at play and in a collaborative frame of mind. Last month I saw Google's lunchroom pictured in *Time* magazine. Employees are encouraged to play Legos and write anything they want on a whiteboard while eating very healthy food. Excellent Factory.

Still and all, we are trying to equip human beings to do something we don't want to do—which is live and thrive in the midst of constant change. It does matter what quality and momentum of change we are talking about. Certainly the notion of having change happen to you is worrying, and it should be. You wish to make change more than react to it. Also, making change in bits exerts a lot of effort and maybe does less good for the trouble than making a lot of change at once. For all these reasons what you often wish to stimulate as a business leader and what is really exciting to participate in is what I call discontinuous change.

THE CASE FOR DISCONTINUOUS CHANGE

Discontinuous change begun in the Institute and perfected in the Factory radically alters the environment and tremendously benefits the authors of it. This is the type of change that visionary business leaders seek out. Americans also happen to be good at it, and, therefore, we should take heart in our ability to thrive in a world of change that we more than anybody else have created.

What is an example of discontinuous change? Consider this story in the rise of the software industry. There were these two guys named Bill and Paul, and they started a company in Phoenix, Arizona, that did something called software. Executives from IBM—which did hardware—came to visit them because the bosses in Armonk said that they needed stuff to put inside the big, shiny, valuable metal boxes that they made.

So the men in the white shirts and ties came to the garage and met the youngsters with the long hair and blue jeans and said, "You seem like nice boys. I understand you have some of this software stuff. Look, we could either buy you out—you look like you could use the money—or we could have a license agreement with you. To tell you the truth, we don't care. What do you guys think? And, oh, this stuff has to have a name for the fellas back at headquarters."

Bill took Paul outside and said, "I can't believe these people. Let's sign the license now before they change their minds."

Paul said, "Well, what are we going to call it?"

Bill said, "I don't know. It is a direct operating system, so why don't we just call it DOS."

And at that moment, all of those people participated in one of the greatest incidents of discontinuous change ever. Instead of buying DOS, IBM licensed it; with that and millions of other licenses, Microsoft came to dominate an industry that few then foresaw. Why was that? Because the valuable thing in the eyes of most everybody were the great, big shiny computers that had the dials, made little noises, and the tape went round and round; you had to get a special room with refrigerators to put them in, and people were very quiet when they worked in there. It was even called hardware. Software, well you know, kids in garages did that.

In business you don't want to be on the wrong side of a moment like that. Now, of course, IBM, after years of change itself, is once again a top company. But being on the wrong side of that moment cost dearly, and now Microsoft is the dominant

The good "Factory" creates environments that keep adults at play and in a collaborative frame of mind. A toy-filled creative space at the Googleplex, Google's headquarters in Mountain View, California, courtesy of Google.

business on the planet. That is one example. There are many others. In short, if you are going to be in a world of change, you must be very alert. A little paranoid even. Out there somewhere is the big change that will alter everything.

You might think that my talk is tilted toward technology businesses or life sciences, where my company operates, when I discuss discontinuous change. And it is true that in knowledge businesses this idea of discontinuous change is quite prevalent. Indeed, part of the genius of Silicon Valley is an ambition to invent whole industries and not stop with individual companies.

For example, when the Internet first blossomed as a communications engine, the partners at Kleiner, Perkins, Caufield, and Byers in Menlo Park said, "Well, why don't we try to start a new industry. Like selling consumer products over the Internet. What goes out first?"

Then the doubts came forth. No one is going to buy things off of a computer. People want to go to stores. Shopping is an experience. All kinds of marketing programs involve getting people in a selling environment. And so on.

So the Kleiner partners said, "Well, let's just start with something small, like books. There is this guy named Jeff who wants to do a company with a strange name—Amazon something." And you know the rest of the story.

Another idea that people now remember nostalgically came to mind when former Governor Mark Warner of Virginia was here giving a talk last month. He made a fortune in the cellular business after practicing law briefly. He told a group that he had saved letters from friends in law school wondering if he had left his senses entirely when he told them his business idea in the 1980s. One after another, they said, "Who is going to want to carry a telephone around?" Another urged him to commit himself to an asylum before it was too late. Well, in the

1980s telephones were large things. You didn't really like carrying them around. But the discontinuous change idea that Governor Warner counted on was being able to make them so they fit comfortably into your pocket. Now everyone carries them around. See, when you think, think big, or in this case, small.

But the fruits of discontinuous change are truly not limited to technology. In the apparel business, for example, we can see it. I was in Vienna in an office building for a meeting, and I saw a young man delivering packages from room to room wearing a Carolina blue T-shirt with a great big UNC Ram on it. I left my group and followed him down the hall, and in a mixture of English and German, I said to him that this was my college, that I had gone to the University of North Carolina. He brightened immediately and said, "Ja, Tar Heels all the way." We talked about his shirt, and apparently it cost him twenty euros that he was very glad to spend. I am told that the UNC logo is the number one selling college logo globally. This is due to the success of the sports teams. But to spread the wealth a very smart law professor in Chapel Hill came up with the idea that 25 percent of the proceeds from university-owned logos should go towards the needy-students scholarship fund.

So what has happened here is a splendid recipe for discontinuous change. Start with a very big idea—something like this: The apparel industry has gone from making garments to being a delivery system for intellectual property. The owners of the intellectual property—in this case well-known American colleges—suddenly have huge margins in a global market licensing their trademarks. The shirt as IP delivery system totally confounds the received wisdom that the apparel business is a low-margin problem. On top of that, the young man who pays twenty euros for a T-shirt in Vienna and enjoys the Tar Heels' athletic success is helping to send a kid from rural North Carolina to school here. I really like that. That is discontinuous change with a social conscience. It is discontinuous change fostered by the type of Institute thinking that makes great leaps, spurred by a very smart law professor who doesn't really work in the field but put her mind to a topic and broke into a whole new reality. Think the Google lunch room.

Institute thinking translates into Factory thinking all of the time in successful businesses. Again, outside of the technology industry and back in apparel, my father's company, Dixie Belle Textiles, for which he has been the Chief Financial Officer for now about forty years and still goes to work every day at the age of eighty—knock on wood—has had a very simple business idea that has allowed it to successfully compete against the Chinese and all comers. If you asked my dad what they do, he says it very simply and to-wit: "We make the cheapest cotton panties any decent woman will wear." Well, now that is funny. It is also a profoundly powerful business idea. Because he and his colleagues in Greensboro can get the design features on such a garment right, they are the preferred providers for Dollar General and Family Dollar and the buyers at Vanity Fair, and they beat out the even cheaper Chinese competition all the time because the Chinese manufacturers, as efficient as they are, do not have that powerful Institute-driven business concept that lets them know what decent American women want in cotton panties. Nor do they have the eye and the design within the price parameters to go into the Factory and get that cultural tone correct.

DISCONTINUOUS CHANGE IN THE POLICY ARENA

A penchant for discontinuous change has served public-policy thinkers well, too. In our better moments in the southern regions, we have embraced heady, drastic change and benefited. There's no better example than the triumph of the Civil Rights Movement, which did nothing if not turn everything upside down. In the economic arena there are good examples, too, none better than putting a global airport in Atlanta, or the establishment of Research Triangle Park in North Carolina in the 1950s, when political, financial, and academic leaders met to follow up on an idea from a local businessman, Romeo Guest, and decided to embark on a corporate and academic research campus in vacant land between major universities. That was a Brave New World concept. It is interesting that forward-thinking companies were among the first to embrace it, because they also saw the now obvious connection early on.

So there is a strong history in the South of successful collaborations among business, academic, and community leaders to bring about progressive change. But this leadership, which V. O. Key, the political scientist from Texas, termed famously the "Progressive Plutocracy," has long been in decline. For a variety of reasons, business leaders have not been as forthcoming and helpful as in earlier times, perhaps simpler times. We've generally been tending to our own nest. Likewise, political leaders have risen from different backgrounds, with different connections, and in a true two-party system. University leaders have had to cope with an unheard-of competitive landscape. Besides that, there is a challenge of sheer scale. It's useful to note generally that several of the southern states, including North Carolina, have doubled in population since the sixties. This influx of different interests and people makes establishing the connections that flourished in the forties, fifties, and sixties more difficult. All of these things make the ease of the old collaborations a difficult challenge indeed.

Beyond that, different times and different voices mean other, more diverse people need to be at the table — the Southern Guy can't take all the seats anymore — and a new transparency doesn't permit doing business so much in private. More diverse representation is proper and good, and transparency admirable. Along the way, however, I think we have managed to erect institutional barriers unintentionally that impede the frank and candid discussion creativity requires. Imagine what getting together a meeting to give birth to the Research Triangle

Park would be like today rather than in 1954. Sadly, I believe that the business leaders wouldn't take time for the meeting because of the press of their quarterly earnings reports; the political leaders would follow advice from their consultants not to be seen with the business people; and the university leaders would try to convert it all into a grant. Meanwhile, everyone would consult their lawyers because the members of the press, if they heard about it, would be trying to discover files under the Public Records Act. All that Governor Luther Hodges, University President Bill Friday, Archie Davis of Wachovia Bank, and Romeo Guest were trying to do that day in 1954 was have lunch. But it's hard to do that kind of lunch anymore. Of course, I simplify a very complicated story. Nonetheless, a more inclusive, more open Progressive Plutocracy needs to work again, much differently and with a new name; and business leaders who are successful in the current global environment have a great deal to offer a new paradigm.

THE UNIVERSITY'S PLACE

One of the most hopeful signs for the future is the emergence in our region of outstanding universities, which are key to so many things, including economic advance. I am reminded of business economist Michael Porter's study of universities as the home to clusters of innovation that drive future wealth. In his view, universities are not simply aiders and abettors of a positive economic climate but are actually the engines of growth themselves. There is a lot to that, and it is hard to argue the contrary in a setting like this; however, the first thing I emphasize about the university's role from the business perspective is actually a more traditional one: universities, both public and private, should focus on what you do best. I think that is teaching kids and making knowledge, each enhancing the other. I have one child in college and another going next year and a third who will come up to it soon, and I want them to be trained to be independent thinkers who don't believe jobs will be given to them but will actively seek and find not one but several careers over their lifetime. Much of this depends upon academic preparation, of course, but also a quality of sheer engagement with the world is really important. Connection to professors who are actively making knowledge in an academic subject encourages optimism, self-reliance, and other things we Americans pride ourselves on. For universities to admit students by rote and teach them by rote, without that connection to making knowledge, will leave us all in a fix, because what this climate of change and more change really leads to is a world in which thinking, independent people have more say than ever before.

This is Tom Friedman's point in his latest book, *The World is Flat*. His view is that the global business organization, which has been a very creative force through the end of the last century, will at some point be eclipsed in power by individual customers and the potential employees who now have faster access to vast stores

The "decent woman" is a mainstay of modern advertising. She is both preferred audience, as with Dixie Belle Textiles's claim that they "make the cheapest cotton panties any decent woman will wear," and subject, as seen here in a late-nineteenth-century advertisement for Acorn Stoves and Ranges, courtesy of the Collections of the Library of Congress.

of information than ever before. This idea is hopeful for those of us grappling in the South with the isolation and real difficulties of some southern working people in the new global economy.

Unfortunately, there is an unbroken connection throughout southern history leading from the plantation to the mill village through the Great Buffalo Hunt of the postwar era that we pay a price for today. That is because there seems to always be a bunch of people who have power who try to decide what the other people who don't have power are going to do. If you want a prescription for disaster in the current world, there it is. We are doing nothing but leading ourselves towards misery if this cycle continues. Leaders from Thomas Jefferson to Martin Luther King have written on how the practice ill serves those in and out of power, creating dependency, false pride, and bad results. In this age of empowerment through information it is completely clear to me that working people in our small towns and in the countryside and in the city alike should require more of their world rather than take what comes, and that education and engagement in a field of knowledge impart a possibility for the future and a desire to demand the life they deserve, rather than accept the one they get. And universities are good at making that happen.

In college I studied the liberal arts. I once had a teacher named Doris Betts who was chair of the UNC-Chapel Hill faculty at one time. Someone asked her what universities are supposed to do. She said, "It's simple; good universities are windows to the world." I agree with that.

Now, let me turn to some practical ways we can better work together. In the life sciences, people like me look at a university's research programs like great big bulletin boards. There are flashing lights everywhere and much noise. We like it, but this frightens us, because in the corporate world, we do everything that we can to eliminate noise. I spend more time than you can imagine trying to make torrents of information flow in the right channels, collecting and managing data so that the Factory or the Institute can consume it efficiently. The orders I give would drive a university faculty crazy. In fact, just imagine me in my job as the Department Chairman from Hell. Keeping a company going has to do with cutting down on noise, but good universities create noise. So there is a tension there, but a necessary one. Keep the noise coming. We'll manage.

Another point has to do with the creative climate of the university community. Richard Florida, in his book *The Rise of the Creative Class*, has noted tellingly that the great economic ideas of our time have come from communities that are happily nonconformist. A tolerant social climate goes far towards encouraging creative thinking of all kinds, most particularly business thinking. The knowledge revolution of this country began in Boston and in Silicon Valley around universities, but more particularly it occurred because of the climate that tolerated difference and celebrated change. Creative failure was and is a badge of pride, not shame. Making a comment as a southerner here, I say that we have a ways to go before the creative class can really truly flourish here in numbers. The universities are our best resources and best hope for change. That is why academic leaders have to hold fast, even in an obsessive way, to notions of academic freedom and to resist any attempts to mute it. Save for clear and present danger to life and limb, there is just really not a good reason to tell a member of the academic community to shut up.

MY DINNER WITH SERGEI

I have spoken about a model of thinking that business leaders can contribute to our discussion. It is a model of living in change while being both innovative and efficient, and making that a habit of mind. It often embraces large change rather than incremental change as a means of creating social and economic value. I have also spoken about the university and tried to give a rather traditional message: that progressive business leaders seek out trained, independent thinkers and creative places for them to live and work. Now I would like to talk a bit about regional and global communities and how the experience of the global business corporation can be illustrative.

When you start a company in different countries the organization goes through several stages of growth. One of my favorite graphs illustrates this point. It was created by Professor George Steiner of Harvard Business School, and he plots the progression of global corporations in this way. First there is an outpost in a foreign country governed totally by directives from the home office. That is a multinational company. Then there are growing foreign enterprises that act semi-autonomously in a federation. That is a transnational company. Finally, there is a truly global company in which there is coequal and robust collaboration among all people wherever they are creating a high level of result within a single business culture. When this is depicted on a graph, the upward arrow stops, showing that the final stage has not yet been reached by any corporation on the planet. It is truly an aspirational goal. But it is notable that it is in the arena of business and not politics or even theology that one finds this form of global community described. We and other companies aspire to it.

Along the way we have built, as people do, a human community that anticipates the organization, and this is where I want to talk about my dinner with Sergei.

Last January I went to Miami for a global meeting of executives in our company. We discussed with each other the progress that we had made and the year ahead; we talked about our goals and our results, and we had a good time. I sat beside Sergei at our closing dinner. Sergei runs our business in Russia. We had a floor show to entertain us. There was rock 'n' roll music, and he knew every eighties song by heart. He discussed with me his children and their schooling in St. Petersburg and how much he loved the city and how he hated to go to Moscow but needed to do it regularly and the traffic was terrible. We talked about our common projects, and I asked him if he liked Miami. "Oh, yes," he said. "The energy, the color, it is so American and it is so fabulous. This is what I always wanted." With that last part, it was as though he were answering more of a question than I had asked, and he suddenly spoke of the travel, the colleagues, the freedom, the rest of it, and we passed a pleasant evening.

I then thought of my friend Gillian who ran our South African business. Gillian was a refugee from Zimbabwe, whose family had a Rhodesian farm, and Xiaomei, who was forced as a child to work in the rice paddies by the Red Guard and now runs our Chinese business. Why did we all like each other so much? Could it be that we all share a heritage of military defeat, economic subjugation, an experience in otherness? And that we like simply to put on a suit and work to our own talents without the baggage of all that?

I read some books about the South when I was in school, and one of them was called *The Burden of Southern History* by C. Vann Woodward. The main part of it—an essay really—was about how we as southerners knew defeat and, therefore, in the American community, we were in the best place to understand the loss of the Vietnam War and the journey of the Vietnamese people. If Woodward, with all of his genius, were writing the essay today, might he call it "The Global Promise of Southern History"? Could that explain my friendships with Sergei and Gillian and Xiaomei and so many others? We need a language to understand this, or a new story about ourselves, because it's not American exceptionalism that my

From cumbersome to ubiquitous, the modern mobile phone is a premier example of discontinuous change. An early mobile phone user, courtesy of Motorola, Inc.

friends around the world identify with, but something more like a country western song.

Whatever they think of us, in their hearts, my friends around the world absolutely expect America to lead. I do think that one thing leadership should bring to bear in this discussion is confidence. In the global world, America has so many advantages. English is the world language. The preferred reserve currency is the dollar and will be as long as our government acts responsibly. American culture is such a powerful draw that it turned six billion people into potential customers, much like the young man in Vienna. People of honesty, intelligence, and drive should be able to seize upon this to make great business enterprises and to think of the world as full of buyers for our goods as well as competitors for our jobs, which they are but which is also beside the point. The laws of economics are not repealed for our friends and rivals either. Even now, those who appear to have advantage are losing it. For example, as I check into the cost of rental for Class A office space in Bangalore, right now it is significantly higher than here in Raleigh/Durham, significantly higher than in Kansas City, and somewhat lower than Los Angeles. That is because demand is high, and it is difficult to build more of it. Some of the advantage of moving to Bangalore doesn't seem as great as it once did.

We can't lead in this world for long by making people afraid. To the contrary, to succeed requires inspiring people to be as good as they are, which is pretty good indeed. One thing that successful businesses try to do is weed out people who lead by fear. That is not because there's nothing to fear, but that it simply is impossible to succeed while being afraid. Organizations may succeed in the short run by scaring people into line, but in this world it doesn't work very long.

I remember a speech by someone who would dearly love this moment in history, a graduate of UNC, Governor, President of Duke University, United States Senator, Terry Sanford. I recall a meeting when he was contemplating his first Senate race. He was speaking to a small group of people, and one of his advisers said to him that he would have to be mindful of those who would attack him as a free trader and soft on communism — still a potent charge in those days — and he would have to campaign accordingly. He got very angry and pounded his fist on the table. He stood up and said, "We are Americans, what are we afraid of? I will not win an election on the backs of workers in Asia or Russian people I don't even know." You want leadership? That's leadership. He won that election. Regrettably, too often in the current environment, politicians try to govern by fear, the media tries to sell the news by fear, and we end up scaring ourselves all the time. It is not that all fear is wrong; it is just that none of it does any good. What the business world brings to the table is the desire to get the best out of everybody, not because that is an admirable thing to do, but because it's what works.

I believe, as William Faulkner said in a more dangerous time and under more difficult circumstances, that human beings will not only endure but prevail. I believe that has a special meaning for us here. From where I sit, there are numerous issues that need to be addressed on the economic front. But the peoples of the American South are so much better off today than ever before. We are richer, freer, more worldly, more relevant. Walker Percy said the South would end when attorneys would rather practice corporate law in Atlanta than New York. Sadly, he didn't live long enough to see Atlanta's offices in London, Brussels, Singapore, or to see New York become an even more powerful global center and truly inviting place to live. The fact is, as the greater world surrounds us, our old national rivalry is now suddenly uninteresting. I think it is useful to remember that in 2006 we are now as far away from the New Deal as the New Deal was from the Civil War. Today the prosperity that visits even the poorest regions in the South is immense by comparison, and the idea that we can have a conference like this in which we think about how to compete in a global economy is a great advance. I do believe, as I remember my dinner with Sergei, that while a larger culture is being born, the southern drama that we've known has picked up and left town. That's the one that begins with the story "We're all born in sin, and then bad things happen and make it worse." It was a great literature, but a lesser life. At some hour near the beginning of this twenty-first century, in the twinkling of an eye, in a moment of discontinuous change, it all vanished. Now, it's gone. There are no plantations, no mill villages. In this new place, we are left with ourselves, and a world to join.

Near Bluffton Mill *and*
Late Spring, Rockfish Gap

HAIKU BY REBECCA LILLY

The Shenandoah Valley from Maryland Heights up to Rockfish Gap (on the north, or right, side of the valley), 1864, by A. R. Ward, courtesy of the Collections of the Library of Congress.

Near Bluffton Mill

1

The old house ruins
Shine with dust; late day coolness
From the pine forest

2

Among the grass tufts
Along a fence: cattle bones . . .
Dry weeds, there again

3

Sawdust and bark chips
In the yard; treetops crackling
As the starlings arc

4

The parched yellow grass
Near a high water mark; sun-
Streaked banks caked with mud

Golden field slopes fade . . .
Hay bales scenting through the boards:
Weathered, flecked with paint

Late Spring, Rockfish Gap

1

On a tree-lined creek bank
Redstarts flutter, hovering,
Darting from birch leaves

After rain: green pastures —
Cloud shapes change at the summit
Through scattered sunbeams

2

At dawn, in the field,
Feathers of a long-eared owl
Float among the stalks

Ripples going outward . . .
Birch twigs drift across water
Where the path runs out

3

On a sunken porch,
An old table and chairs; wasps
Buzz through weathered doors

The horse pasture warms . . .
Some mist-wrapped morning glories
Open through fence boards

Ed. Note: The haiku is an ancient Japanese form noted for its ability to capture landscape and emotion in a very short space. It seemed an intriguing act of globalization to apply the form to Bluffton Mill and the creeks and trees of Rockfish Gap.

"In My Heart, I'm an American"

Regional Attitudes and American Identity

BY LARRY J. GRIFFIN AND KATHERINE MCFARLAND

As the essays in this issue of *Southern Cultures* confirm, it is now old news to point to the changing demographic face of the South. We all know that immigration is transforming the region, that newcomers—new southerners, to be sure, but also new *kinds* of southerners—are introducing novel ways of speaking, of eating, of worshiping. These cultural innovations bring new diversity to a place long noted for its starkly black and white biracialism, its ethnically homogenous Anglo-Celtic whites, and its Christ-haunted Protestantism. Of course, as any number of Chinese in Mississippi, French-speaking Cajuns in Louisiana, Jews in South Carolina, German Lutherans in Texas, and Catholics in Maryland will tell us, the South has always housed more cultural diversity than the above generalizations allow, and it is much too simple to say that southerners are entirely unfamiliar with the voluntary and involuntary flow of people into the region from near and distant shores. Yet these generalizations nonetheless hold much truth: even today, the ancestry of most southerners points to Africa or the British Isles. Still, for most of its history, Dixie lagged way behind the rest of the country in terms of attracting immigrants and thus has far less experience with such perennial "American" themes as ethnic and religious nativism, assimilation, and pluralism.[1]

That all of this is now rapidly changing raises huge questions about both public policy and public morality—questions about Americanism and southernism, about inclusion and exclusion, questions, ultimately, about that most elemental of national matters, who "we" are and who "we" permit to become part of "us." Past South Polls have explored these questions of southern exceptionalism using the Southern Focus Poll, an annual survey of the UNC Odum Institute for Research in Social Science conducted between 1992 and 2001. Recent public data, taken largely from the General Social Surveys (GSS) in 1996 and 2004, offer new information on the attitudes and opinions of representative Americans, differentiated by region, about these issues. Because many of the same questions were asked in both years, the GSS is especially useful for gauging change in how Americans answer the question about what it means to be an American and in their opinions of immigration and immigrants. Comparing southerners with nonsoutherners also reveals the degree of regional divergence or convergence in these attitudes.[2]

According to the idealistic political understanding of America, part of the nation's mission—however insufficiently realized in practice, policy, and law—has always been as beacon and magnet to the world's downtrodden and despised. No other country has become home to so many immigrants, and to so many different kinds of immigrants. New arrivals at Ellis Island, New York, 1908, from the Records of the Public Health Service, courtesy of the National Archives.

WHAT DOES IT MEAN TO BE AMERICAN?

No fixed consensus exists as to what it means to be an American because the definition of America and thus of American identity itself are the subject of heated debate, negotiation, and conflict. On the one hand, liberal, idealistic definitions of America assert that the United States, unique among modern nations, is not premised on a common ethnicity, race, language, religion, or even homeland, and what makes Americans "Americans"—that is, why we have the particular national identity we do—is not rooted in any of these things, either. Rather, these definitions hold that both the nation and American identity rest on an explicit ideological understanding of a people and the state they created. America and Americans, then, are assumed to be defined politically—that is, by a set of political ideals assumed universal in their applicability—rather than culturally, or, in the words of historian Arthur Mann, by "the bond of common paternity."[3]

Vernacular or "folk" definitions of American identity, on the other hand, which in earlier times were often entangled with "official" definitions issued by governments at all levels, generally assert the opposite; that America is in fact grounded not in abstract political ideals but in "culture" and quite concrete cultural markers: in a particular ethnicity or race (European, especially northwestern European), in a particular language (English), and in a particular religion (Christianity, especially

Protestantism). Such folk definitions of American identity have bred solidarity and a sense of unity and purpose among those sharing these ascriptive (race, ethnicity) and "achieved" (English speaking, Protestant) attributes, but frequently at the expense of those—immigrants and Americans alike—with different ethnicities, tongues, and faiths. Adherents to this definition therefore believe American identity to be quite clearly and properly stamped by cultural particularism rather than political universalism. Much of U.S. history is the consequence of the interplay between these two definitions.

All of the above suggest that American identity is an example of what philosophers call an "essentially contested concept"—one whose meaning cannot be fixed by an appeal to evidence or logic and thus is subject to endless dispute. Nonetheless, the line separating the idealistic, political definition of American identity from the folk, cultural definition has not always been as sharp as may first appear.

The idealistic base of the liberal, political view of American identity, according to the Swedish economist Gunnar Myrdal in his magisterial analysis of American race relations, *An American Dilemma*, espouses "the essential dignity of the individual human being, the fundamental equality of all men, and . . . certain inalienable rights of freedom, justice, and a fair opportunity." Advanced in Colonial America as early as the 1760s, this political definition, seen perhaps most eloquently in the Declaration of Independence, is at the heart of what Myrdal famously called "The American Creed" and, again in liberal, idealistic definitions of American identity, both empowers and obligates all Americans with its normative force; this, Myrdal seems to be saying, is what Americans, as a people and as a nation, ideally ought to be, what we should aspire to be.[4]

In Myrdal's thinking, though, the American Creed bears even more weight than this—much more. He says that the creed "is identified with America's peculiar brand of nationalism," thus serving to give Americans their sense of "historical mission," a fact, he suggests, of global significance. According to this idealistic political understanding of America, part of that mission—however superseded it may be by cultural definitions of American identity and thus however insufficiently realized in practice, policy, and law—has always been as beacon and magnet to the world's downtrodden and despised. Remember the Statue of Liberty with its famous poem written in 1883 by Emma Lazarus: "Keep, ancient lands, your storied pomp! . . . Give me your tired, your poor, your huddled masses, yearning to breathe free." No other country, historian Mann tells us, has become home to so many immigrants, and to so many different kinds of immigrants, most of whom were drawn by a promise enshrined in the creed.[5]

Going further still, Myrdal argues that because Americans have no commonality rooted in what usually constitutes a "folk" or a distinct people—such as language, religion, a homeland, and so on—then something external, something independent of culture in this sense of the term, must serve as the indispensable social adhesive. So he considers the creed to be the political glue holding a culturally diverse and pluralistic people—a nation of immigrants—together. Americans, from this definition, thus need no common culture, no common paternity; they need simply to bind themselves to the creed and thereby to each other.

Myrdal also sees the creed as satisfying yet another crucial social function. Though Americans, in his view, "ought" to act in a creedal fashion, we oft-times do not, thereby falling short of our highest ideals. And history does tell us that we have all too frequently fallen short—and this is painfully true for white southerners—precisely in forgetting that no race, no ethnicity, no religion, no language "owns" America or defines American identity. The United States' past is replete with racial, ethnic, and religious persecution and exclusion, both state-sponsored or -sanctioned and otherwise. Among the many examples of this are the Naturalization Act of 1790, which employed explicitly racial criteria limiting citizenship in this nation to "free white persons"; the Indian Removal Act of 1824; the Chinese Exclusion Acts of the 1880s; and the Executive Order 9066, which authorized the mass incarceration of over 110,000 Japanese Americans in so-called "internment" camps during World War II, an order signed by the very man who a year earlier had delivered his famous, profoundly creedal "Four Freedoms" speech, President Franklin D. Roosevelt.

Much of this was a direct consequence of white supremacy, overt racism, and various prejudices against a strange or foreign "other." But some of the distance separating creed from deed—as our collective moral "lapses" are sometimes called by those adherents of the idealistic political understanding of American identity—stems from real, if wrenchingly misguided, fears for the very idea of "America." Here is one area where the political and cultural definitions of American identity interweave. Because Americans are a hugely diverse people who share only a political definition of who we are—a common ancestral culture is neither necessary nor obtainable in this country—adherence to the creed is essential for national unity, and so throughout our history we have occasionally obsessed about the loyalties and allegiances of immigrants, and even of American citizens whose ethnicity or language or religion stamped them as somehow "different" from most Americans or most southerners.

In the event of war, we ask ourselves, will "they" align themselves with their ancestral homelands against America? Will their attempts to keep alive their culture and language fracture America? To whom and to what are they loyal—to their particularistic culture, whatever that may be, or to the creedal political abstraction that is America? During the 1960 presidential campaign, for example, prominent Protestant clergy, led by the Reverend Norman Vincent Peale, questioned "the loyalty of any Catholic candidate for president and the wisdom of choosing any man of that faith for the high office," forcing John F. Kennedy both to declare

U.S. history is replete with racial, ethnic, and religious persecution and exclusion, both state-sanctioned and otherwise. President Franklin D. Roosevelt's Executive Order 9066, for instance, authorized the mass incarceration of over 110,000 Japanese Americans in so-called "internment" camps during World War II, an order signed a year after his famous and profoundly creedal "Four Freedoms" speech. Children pledging allegiance at Weill Public School in San Francisco, 1942, prior to their relocation to an internment camp, courtesy of the Collections of the Library of Congress.

before the Greater Houston Ministerial Association that he did not speak for his church and his church did not speak for him, and to proclaim his commitment to the separation of church and state and to religious tolerance and pluralism. The creed, in a particular way, thus lends itself to this sort of hyperpatriotic abuse: although its logic is one of universalism, its geographic impetus, as Myrdal has shown, is highly particularistic, largely limited to northwestern Europe, and so the bigoted and fearful amongst us can use its Protestant, Eurocentric roots to express the exclusionary folk or cultural definition of American identity.[6]

How does America come to understand and ultimately repudiate its own racism, ethnocentrism, and xenophobia — to make right its wrongs? To Myrdal and other advocates of a political definition of America, the answer is simple: the creed — or, at least, social movements of the dispossessed and disfranchised inspired by and armed with the universalism of the creed. So in addition to doing all the other important things already discussed, the creed also serves, again in the words of Myrdal, as the "American Conscience" — the moral standard we use to judge the goodness or badness of our practices, our laws, and our institutions, the yardstick that tells us how far we must go to realize the high political ideals upon which the nation, and American identity, were founded.

The creed, though, lacks the visceral appeal of ethnic or religious commonality, and so the political definition of American identity is constantly challenged by the cultural definition. Even in recent times, particularism can trump universalism, not only among everyday folk but among public officials as well. At a meeting of Republican governors in 1992, then Mississippi Governor Kirk Fordice proclaimed that the United States "was a Christian nation, which," he added, "does not mean in any way to infer any kind of religious intolerance or any kind of particular dogma that is being forced on anyone. It's just a simple fact of life in the United States of America." Tying what he saw as the defining quality of the nation to its potential downfall, Fordice then added, "And the less we emphasize the Christian religion, the further we fall into the abyss of poor character and chaos." When another southern governor, Carroll A. Campbell of South Carolina, tried to broaden the religious character of the United States by adding "Judeo-" to "Christian," Fordice said, "If I had wanted to do that, I would have done it." Similar sentiments fueled former Alabama Supreme Court Chief Justice Roy Moore's losing efforts to place a Ten Commandments monument in his courtroom. More secular appeals to cultural particularism, emphasizing, again, the threat to the creed and to national unity, come from the learned and influential, notably Harvard political scientist Samuel Huntington and CNN's Lou Dobbs, both of whom fear that unacculturated immigrants from Latin America will mortally wound American national identity. Such anxieties are also repeatedly heard on the floor of the U.S. Congress. For example, during a 2006 debate on immigration in which the U.S. Senate voted 63-34 to make English the official language in the United States (the bill was never put into law), Republican Senator Lamar Alexander from Tennessee argued that "English is part of our national identity. It's part of our spirit. It's part of our blood. It's part of who we are." Clearly, the cultural definition of America is alive and well, illustrating, once more, that no societal agreement on American identity exists.[7]

Cultural pluralism and the subject that fuels much of the debate about it, immigration, thus again seem to be hot-button issues, and we have little good evidence for what Americans currently think about "Americanism"—that is, about what it means to be an American. Now that the United States contains, as sociologist Alan Wolfe puts it, more "nonwhite people whose first language is not English" than at any point in its history, Americans are being challenged to define our national identity and to articulate just how inclusive we are to be. Perhaps the firmest conclusion to be reached regarding what Americans believe about immigration is that we, collectively and individually, are likely confused, most certainly conflicted. Many Americans appear distressed by the way immigration is handled in the United States today, even as they value the contributions of immigrants to the nation. A slight plurality (43 percent) of Americans, polled in April 2007 by USA Today/Gallup, for instance, believed that the United States has "lost ground" in dealing with illegal immigration in the past year; only 12 percent felt that the country has made progress. But while a majority of Americans (54 percent), also surveyed in April 2007 by the *Los Angeles Times*/Bloomberg Poll, believed that illegal immigrants harm the nation's economy, 55 percent preferred a guest-worker program in conjunction with tougher border enforcement to a strategy emphasizing only enforcement (40 percent). Likewise, most Americans (78 percent), asked in April 2007 by USA Today/Gallup about a number of ways to handle the problem of illegal immigrants in the United States, chose policies permitting a path toward citizenship rather than those that called for deportation, either with (only 6 percent supported) or without (14 percent supported) a chance to return.[8]

Illegal immigration is but the tip of the iceberg: 55 percent of Americans, when polled by Gallup in early 2007, said that the overall level of immigration should be decreased, up from 45 percent in January 2001; the percent of those who believed it should be increased was in the single digits. The Gallup Poll also found, in June 2006, that almost half of all Americans polled thought immigration from Latin America should be curtailed. Is this evidence of a new nativism, of renewed (if possibly passing) intolerance and exclusion? How pervasive is the creedal understanding of American identity, a national identity premised on political ideals rather than culture? Conversely, do many Americans embrace a cultural underpinning of "us," one that places ancestry, language, and ethnicity above those ideals?

REGIONAL DIFFERENCES AND THE CREED

American opinions gathered by the General Social Survey can shed new light on these questions and on any regional differences that may exist. In both 1996 and 2004, the GSS asked respondents the following question: "Some people say the following things are important for being truly American. Others say they are not important. How important do you think each of the following is?" In 1996 seven characteristics were queried; in 2004, eight. For each trait, respondents were asked if it was "very important," "fairly important," "not very important," or "not at all important." A residual category, "can't choose," was volunteered by a small percent of respondents (0.5 to 3 percent). The traits and the percent of Americans believing each "very important" is seen in Table 1. We report the results separately for three regional groups of respondents: a) those who are lifelong residents of the South; b) those who either grew up in the South but now live elsewhere ("exiles") or grew up elsewhere but now live in the South ("transplants"); and c) lifelong nonsoutherners. (We combine exiles and transplants because, separately, there are too few of either in the sample to permit reliable interpretation.)[9]

Table 1: Americans' Opinions About the Traits Necessary for Being "Truly American" (1996 and 2004 General Social Surveys)

	% Responding "Very Important"			
	Lifelong Southerners	Exiles/ Transplants	Lifelong Nonsoutherners	Total Sample
To have American citizenship				
1996	84	75	71	75
2004	87	77	81	82
To respect America's political institutions/laws				
1996	70	64	61	63
2004	72	72	71	72
To feel American				
1996	70	61	57	61
2004	72	64	65	67
To have American ancestry				
2004	44	25	28	32
To have lived in America for most of one's life				
1996	57	46	38	44
2004	69	47	56	58
To have been born in America				
1996	57	38	34	40
2004	68	45	53	56
To be able to speak English				
1996	78	71	68	71
2004	88	85	81	83
To be a Christian				
1996	57	40	29	38
2004	63	47	42	48
Number of respondents, 1996*				
	346–350	164–165	834–838	1,344–1,351
Number of respondents, 2004*				
	329–330	142	742–743	1,213–1,215

*The number of respondents generally varied by question.

Southern cultures

For fastest service, please call [919] 966-3561, ext. 256, Monday–Friday between 8:00 a.m. and 3:00 p.m. EST with credit card information or fax your order to [800] 272-6817. You can also send e-mail to uncpress_journals@unc.edu.

INDIVIDUAL subscription request

Please enter my subscription to *Southern Cultures* at the rate of $28 for four quarterly issues. [Add $12 for postage outside the US.] *This price is good until December 31, 2007.*

❑ My check or money order, payable to THE UNIVERSITY OF NORTH CAROLINA PRESS, is enclosed in an envelope with this card.

❑ Please charge my Visa or MasterCard [circle one].

CARD NUMBER _____ EXP. DATE _____

SIGNATURE _____ DAYTIME PHONE _____

NAME _____

ADDRESS _____ ZIP CODE _____

Southern cultures

For fastest service, please call [919] 966-3561, ext. 256, Monday–Friday between 8:00 a.m. and 3:00 p.m. EST with credit card information or fax your order to [800] 272-6817. You can also send e-mail to uncpress_journals@unc.edu.

INSTITUTION subscription request

Please enter my subscription to *Southern Cultures* at the rate of $52.50 for four quarterly issues. [Add $12 for postage outside the US.] *This price is good until December 31, 2007.*

❑ My check or money order, payable to THE UNIVERSITY OF NORTH CAROLINA PRESS, is enclosed in an envelope with this card.

❑ Please charge my Visa or MasterCard [circle one].

CARD NUMBER _____ EXP. DATE _____

SIGNATURE _____ DAYTIME PHONE _____

NAME _____

ADDRESS _____ ZIP CODE _____

BUSINESS REPLY MAIL
FIRST-CLASS MAIL   PERMIT NO. 509   CHAPEL HILL, NC

POSTAGE WILL BE PAID BY ADDRESSEE

THE UNIVERSITY OF NORTH CAROLINA PRESS
JOURNALS FULFILLMENT
116 S BOUNDARY STREET
CHAPEL HILL, NC 27514-9943

NO POSTAGE
NECESSARY
IF MAILED
IN THE
UNITED STATES

BUSINESS REPLY MAIL
FIRST-CLASS MAIL   PERMIT NO. 509   CHAPEL HILL, NC

POSTAGE WILL BE PAID BY ADDRESSEE

THE UNIVERSITY OF NORTH CAROLINA PRESS
JOURNALS FULFILLMENT
116 S BOUNDARY STREET
CHAPEL HILL, NC 27514-9943

NO POSTAGE
NECESSARY
IF MAILED
IN THE
UNITED STATES

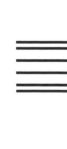

Consider, first, those attributes of "true Americanism" that are creedal in nature, or at least do not represent an open break with a culturally inclusive, political definition of American identity. The vast majority of Americans believed both in 1996 and in 2004 that having American citizenship (71 to 87 percent) and respecting the nation's political institutions and laws (61 to 72 percent) were "very important" to be "truly American." Lifelong southerners, more than others, were a bit stricter here, but by 2004 these differences were small or nonexistent. Regional differences are also small in 2004 for the trait "feel like an American" as well, with a majority of all three groups believing this subjective state of genuine import. These "requirements"—or so they are viewed by large percentages of Americans—do not seem unduly constraining or exclusionary, though one could argue that some laws and political institutions deserve more respect than others. Nevertheless, none of these attributes courts overtly cultural requirements of "true Americanism." The same, however, cannot be said for the next five components queried: American ancestry, longtime residence in the United States, American birth, English-speaking, and Christian. All of these, in one way or another, would impose quite stringent ethnic, linguistic, or religious criteria on the ability of many in this nation—most of whom are its citizens—to claim or assert a "real" or "true" American identity.

Significantly larger percentages of all regional groups in 2004 than in 1996 state that four of the five explicitly particularistic or ascriptive—exclusionary, in any case—components of true Americanism are "very important." The sole exception to this generalization is that exiles/transplants did not believe having lived in America for most of one's life more important from one survey to the other. (The fifth trait, American ancestry, was not queried in 1996.) Though we have no systematic data on why we see these attitudinal changes from 1996 to 2004, it is possible that 9/11, the "war on terror," and the current Iraq war—all of which were on prominent public display during the 2004 presidential campaign—play an important role in what is an increasingly narrow popular understanding of Americanism. Such an inference is certainly consistent with the heightened number of attacks against Arab Americans and Muslim Americans after 9/11.[10]

The majority of Americans in 2004—sweeping majorities, in one case—believe most of these attributes "very important" (see the "Total Sample" column in Table 1). Only for American ancestry does a clear minority of those polled believe this, and even here, 54 percent of all Americans (irrespective of region) believe it either "very important" or "fairly important." (Percentages for the "fairly important" category do not appear in Table 1). Fifty-six percent believed it very important to have been born in America to be "truly American," and another 20 percent asserted it was "fairly important." Similarly, 80 percent thought having lived in America for most of one's life either very or fairly important (58 percent

Despite all the theorizing about what it means to be an American by intellectuals and politicians, vernacular or folk expressions of American identity are not underpinned by universal, inclusive political ideals but, instead, by particularistic and exclusionary, ancestral, linguistic, and religious criteria, the sort of standard most immigrants would of necessity fail. Department of Labor training service class in English and citizenship for Italian immigrants, Newark, New Jersey, ca. 1925, courtesy of the Collections of the Library of Congress.

said it was very important). Eighty-three percent thought speaking English very important; add to that the additional 14 percent who replied that it was fairly important, and we have, in 2004, 97 percent of a representative sample of Americans willing to say in a public poll that an inability to speak English effectively rendered "true Americanism" unlikely, perhaps even impossible. Even more exclusionary in their logic are the statistics pertaining to the import of being a Christian: a near-majority of Americans, 48 percent, believed identifying with this particularistic faith very important, and another 16 percent answered fairly important. Almost two-thirds of these respondents, then, think being a Christian at least of some significance for "true Americanism."

One statistic (not included in Table 1) does offer evidence of a contrary sentiment. Both the 1996 GSS and 2004 GSS included a question asking if respondents agreed with the statement, "It is impossible for people who do not share American customs and traditions to become fully American." They could answer either "strongly agree," "agree," "neither agree nor disagree," "disagree," or "disagree strongly." The modal response in both years was "disagree," with 33 percent of Americans choosing it in 1996 and 36 percent in 2004. Only about a third either "strongly agreed" or "agreed" in either 1996 or 2004. But it is not entirely clear how to interpret these results, especially given the tightly systematic pattern seen with the "truly American" characteristics in Table 1. The question is phrased in terms of a double negative ("impossible," "do not share"), which can confuse respondents. Moreover, when we look at the responses to this question of only those polled who believed the ability to speak English "very important," we do see more exclusionary responses (data not shown). Nonetheless, here, at least, we see much lower levels of particularism. However, these responses, when taken together, strongly indicate that despite all the theorizing about what it means to be an American by intellectuals and politicians, as late as 2004 vernacular or folk expressions of American identity were not underpinned by universal, inclusive political ideals but instead by particularistic, ancestral, linguistic, and religious criteria, the sort of standard most immigrants would of necessity fail.

Table 1 also shows fairly large regional differences in American assertions of the importance of the more restrictive identity attributes. Lifelong residents of nonsouthern environs more closely resemble their peers in Dixie in 2004 than in 1996—meaning that "northerners" have moved more rapidly down the path of restriction than have long-term southerners. Though hardly constituting proof, this is consistent with the argument, offered by such perceptive South-watchers as John Egerton and Peter Applebome, that the region is transforming the United States in its own image. But, nonetheless, as of 2004 it is lifelong southerners who consistently remain most particularistic and exclusionary, with exiles and transplants usually closer to the beliefs of respondents who have never lived below the Mason-Dixon Line. Differences in the percentages of lifelong southerners and nonsoutherners who believed these traits are very important range, in 2004, from 7 percent for being able to speak English (88 percent v. 81 percent) to 21 percent for being a Christian (63 percent v. 42 percent). That so many lifelong southerners believe that one must be a Christian to be truly American may be due to the region's long-standing religious homogeneity: for many southerners of all races, a Christian America is the only America they know. Whatever the exact reason, though, these responses do suggest that the Mississippian Kirk Fordice, the Alabamian Roy Moore, and the Tennessean Lamar Alexander represented a great many of their coregionalists' sectarian beliefs.[11]

Averaging across responses to the five most restrictive characteristics in Table 1 (from having American ancestry through being a Christian), we find that a bit more than half of lifelong nonsoutherners (52 percent) in 2004 believe these traits very important to being "truly American"; two-thirds of lifelong southerners do. Additionally, an average of 80 percent of the latter said these five characteristics are either "very" or "fairly" important; sometimes, as in the case of having lived most of one's life in the South and the importance of speaking English, the percentages approach or exceed 90. Except for English-speaking ability, which almost all of each group believe either very or fairly important (these data are not shown), the differences between "lifers" in the other regions and the South range from 6 percent (long-term residency in the United States) to 29 percent

Figure 1. Regional Differences in Culturally Restrictive "True American" Traits

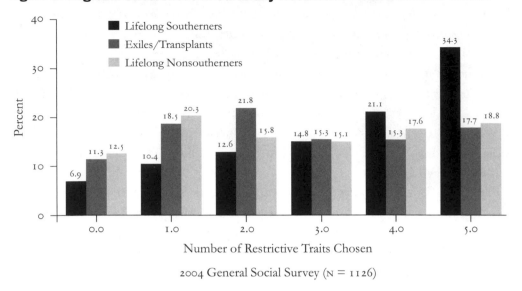

2004 General Social Survey (N = 1126)

(Christian). Another way to see the magnitude of these regional differences is to calculate the percentage of each of the three regional groups who believe that one, two, three, four, or all five of the most particularistic characteristics are very important (see Figure 1). In 2004 only one in six lifelong southerners judge that a small of number of these traits—none or only one—is very important (17 percent); 30 percent or more of exiles and transplants do so, as do one in three lifelong nonsoutherners. Likewise, only a third or so of the latter two groups attribute great importance to a large number—four or all five—of these particularistic characteristics; more than half (55 percent) of Dixie's permanent residents do so. If, in recent times, Americans generally have become more exclusionary in their conceptions of American identity, southerners, at least those who have lived in the region for most of their lives (and they are the most numerous of Dixie's denizens), appear to have led the way.[12]

REGIONAL DIFFERENCES IN THE PERCEPTION OF IMMIGRANTS

While beliefs about what it means to be an American are no doubt intimately tied to attitudes about immigration, it does not necessarily follow that because southerners and other Americans are ungenerous in their estimation of Americanism's requirements they therefore hate or fear immigrants. It is one thing to posit particularistic criteria for "true" Americanism; it is quite another to judge and damn human beings, even those who remain largely unknown to most Americans. So what are the recent American opinions about the latest influx of newcomers, and how have these attitudes changed in the recent past? Are these opinions equally shared by southerners and nonsoutherners?

The GSS asked respondents the degree to which they agreed or not with a series of positive and negative assertions about immigrants and their impact on America. Each of the statements was prefaced by the assertion, "There are different opinions about immigrants from other countries living in America." (See Table 2 for statements.) Each statement permitted respondents five alternatives: "strongly agree," "agree," "neither agree nor disagree," "disagree," and "strongly disagree." In Table 2 we present the percentage of respondents who both strongly agreed or agreed and those who disagreed or strongly disagreed by regional group. The remaining percentage of respondents, not shown in the table, neither agreed nor disagreed with the statement.

American assessments of the consequences of immigration, at least as we can gauge them from the three statements asked in both surveys, are both more positive and less negative in 2004 than in 1996, regardless of region. More respondents both a) agree or strongly agree that immigrants are good for America in the more recent survey, and b) disagree or strongly disagree that they cause higher crime rates or take jobs away from Americans. For example, between one-third and one-half of Americans surveyed in 2004 said that immigrants are good for America (depending on region), and greater numbers judged that they improve American society (as high as 71 percent for exiles/transplants). While many believe that immigrants harm the United States by causing higher crime rates (25 to 31 percent) or by taking American jobs (40 to 52 percent), these percentages are down from 1996. So even as most Americans appear to embrace increasingly exclusionary interpretations of American identity, they also claim to have more positive views of immigrants in 2004 than eight years previously. This seems paradoxical, and to the extent that both sets of findings broadly map the true beliefs of the GSS respondents, they intimate that Americans, again both as a collectivity and as individuals, are confused or conflicted about what they think of the country's newcomers and the changes they have brought. Public opinion about immigration no doubt is to a degree fluid, a function of political initiatives and local, situational factors. Alternatively, these seemingly contradictory patterns may indicate that "we" have loosened the tether between Americanism, on the one hand, and immigration, on the other. Yes, we seem to say, immigration is better for the nation than "we" once thought, but some immigrants — those, for example, who do not speak English or are not Christian — still may not be qualified to be "true" Americans. Note, too, that the notion of "better" is ambiguous here: respondents may interpret this to mean that immigrants bring with them new ideas or innovative, useful cultural patterns, or they may believe that because immigrants frequently occupy low-wage jobs, the latter thus "better" the United States.

The GSS also shows that there is little consensus among Americans about the recent effects of immigration (see the "total sample" row under each statement). Paradoxically, only for views about whether "the government spends too much

**Table 2: Americans' Opinions About Immigrants' Impact on America
(1996 and 2004 General Social Surveys)**

	Percent Responding			
	1996		2004	
	SA/A*	SD/D*	SA/A*	SD/D*
Immigrants Are Good for America				
Lifelong Southerners	23	45	33	32
Exiles/Transplants	44	29	50	21
Lifelong Nonsoutherners	36	29	50	22
Total Sample	34	33	45	25
Immigrants Improve American Society with New Ideas/Cultures				
Lifelong Southerners	NA		44	26
Exiles/Transplants	NA		71	14
Lifelong Nonsoutherners	NA		60	16
Total Sample	NA		57	18
Immigrants Should Have Same Legal Rights as Americans				
Lifelong Southerners	NA		37	47
Exiles/Transplants	NA		36	49
Lifelong Nonsoutherners	NA		40	45
Total Sample	NA		39	46
Government Spends Too Much Money on Immigrants				
Lifelong Southerners	NA		58	14
Exiles/Transplants	NA		48	27
Lifelong Nonsoutherners	NA		50	24
Total Sample	NA		52	21
Immigrants Cause Higher Crimes Rates				
Lifelong Southerners	45	26	31	35
Exiles/Transplants	31	44	27	51
Lifelong Nonsoutherners	29	41	25	47
Total Sample	33	38	27	44
Immigrants Take Jobs Away				
Lifelong Southerners	63	19	52	25
Exiles/Transplants	41	34	41	36
Lifelong Nonsoutherners	44	31	40	38
Total Sample	48	29	43	34
Number of respondents**	1,250–1,281		1,179–1,200	

*SA/A = "Strongly Agree" or "Agree"; SD/D = "Strongly Disagree" or "Disagree."
The remaining percentage of respondents answered "Neither Agree nor Disagree."
**The number of respondents varied by question.

money" on immigrants and if immigration improves the United States does a true majority opinion exist in 2004: 52 percent say immigrants cost too much and 57 percent believe that they improve American society. For the remaining four statements, public opinion is deeply divided. This, as well as the fact that any consensus that does exist appears paradoxical, simultaneously pulling in opposite directions, only exacerbates extant political difficulties in reaching consensus on how the nation should handle immigration.

Important regional differences in these opinions continue. Lifelong southerners are appreciably more particularistic in their understanding of what it means to be an American than are other folks in the United States (see Table 1); so, too, are they harsher in their judgments of immigrants, even in 2004 when their opinions are closer to the mainstream (see Table 2). They less frequently agree with positive assessments of immigration and more frequently disagree with them (immigrants are good for, and improve, America); moreover, they more often agree with negative evaluations and less often disagree with them (immigrants cause high crime rates, take jobs away). In 2004, for instance, only a third of lifelong southerners said that immigrants are good for America; half of the exiles/transplants and lifelong nonsoutherners asserted this. Likewise, 44 percent of lifelong southerners, compared to 71 percent of exiles/transplants and 60 percent of lifelong nonsoutherners, thought immigrants "improve" America.

Another way to look at these patterns is to note that only 36 percent of lifelong southerners believe two or all three of the positive sentiments about immigrants (they are good for/improve America, deserve legal rights) compared to 57 percent of exiles/transplants and 53 percent of lifelong nonsoutherners. Similarly, more of Dixie's lifelong residents also agree or strongly agree with more of the negative assessments (immigrants cost too much money, cause higher crime rates, take jobs away): 47 percent of them believe two or three of the negative views compared to 35 percent of the two other groups who do so. Overall, then, we see more disapproval and condemnation of immigration, and less generous appraisals of immigrants themselves, among Americans who have spent their entire lives in the South.[13]

In 1996, 2004, and 2006 the GSS asked respondents if they thought the "number of immigrants to America nowadays should be" increased a lot, increased a little, remain the same as it is now, reduced a little, or reduced a lot. Consistent with the increasingly positive view of immigrants seen in Table 2, American opinions liberalized between 1996 and 2006. (See the "total sample" row in Table 3.) Nonetheless, as of the latter date, a clear majority of Americans, 53 percent, continue to prefer a reduction in the level of immigration; only 13 percent expressed a wish for an increase in immigration. (Roughly equal numbers of respondents answered "decreased a lot" and "decreased a little.") The remainder (35 percent in 2006) preferred that the number of immigrants remain constant. For every American in

Table 3: Americans' Preferences About the Volume of Immigration (1996, 2004, and 2006 General Social Surveys)

	Lifelong Southerners	Exiles/ Transplants	Lifelong Nonsoutherners	Total Sample
Percent Responding That the Number of Immigrants Should Be Increased*				
1996	7	10	9	9
2004	8	17	10	10
2006	10	17	13	13
Percent Responding That the Number of Immigrants Should Be Decreased**				
1996	72	61	62	64
2004	62	51	53	55
2006	62	44	50	53

*Percent preferring either "increased a lot" or "increased a little."
**Percent preferring either "decreased a lot" or "decreased a little."
The remaining percentage of respondents answered "Remain the Same As It Is Now."
N of Respondents, 1996 = 1,141
N of Respondents, 2004 = 1,983
N of Respondents, 2006 = 1,945

the 2006 GSS who wished to increase the flow of in-migration a lot or even a little, four wished to decrease it; for every American who wished to increase immigration "a lot," more than seven wished to decrease it "a lot."

By 2004 the GSS data show few robust regional differences in attitudes about a) government assistance to ethnic minorities (most Americans said no), b) racial and ethnic distinctiveness versus assimilation (most Americans preferred the latter), c) the exclusion of illegal immigrants (70 percent believed they should be excluded), and d) the status of parents with children born in the United States (75 percent believed that such parents should be permitted to become citizens). Regional differences in anti-immigrant sentiment, however, are considerable (see Table 3): in 2006 lifelong southerners, when compared to the other two groups, preferred by a margin of 12 percent (compared to lifelong nonsoutherners) and 18 percent (compared to exiles/transplants) that the volume of immigration be reduced. Ten percent of "lifers" believed immigration should be increased; more than 60 percent believed it should be decreased. No doubt many factors affect how people feel about this issue, but the sort of positive and negative evaluations of immigrants discussed above probably play a role here: those who believe immigrants are good for the country are likely to be more welcoming of newcomers; those who see immigrants as harmful—and lifelong southerners do so more than other Americans (see Table 2)—are likely to wish to staunch the flow of immigrants. This, as can be seen in Table 3, is in fact the pattern we find.[14]

Even as most Americans appear to embrace increasingly exclusionary interpretations of American identity, they also claim to have more positive views of immigrants than eight years previously, a seemingly paradoxical perspective—but one with a longstanding history in the country, evident, for example, both in the Chinese Exclusion Acts of the 1880s and the government's appeals to new immigrants by evoking the Creed in its World War I posters (here). Courtesy of the Collections of the Library of Congress.

Virtually all these data on Americanism and immigration consistently indicate that those who have deeply imbibed southern culture generally hold both more exclusionary views of what makes an individual a true American and less charitable opinions of immigrants than do other Americans. And the more of the culture we have imbibed, seemingly the more narrow and harsh the attitudes. It is not a matter of simply having lived in the South as an adolescent, nor, after migrating here, living in the region as an adult. After all, exiles and transplants—both of which have had exposure to the South and its social arrangements—are frequently more inclusive in their sense of American identity and appreciative of immigrants than are lifelong nonsoutherners. It is, instead, lifelong southerners who advance more restrictive immigration policies than do others because, in part at least, they both evaluate immigrants more negatively and are more apt to understand "Americanism" in more restrictive ways. More than other regional groups, those of us who have lived here all our lives define what it means to be an American with the imagery of ancestry, language, religion, and paternity—exactly opposite, one could argue, what the American Creed calls for, exactly opposite what an open, pluralistic, diverse multicultural region and nation require.

Why do we see such consistent regional patterns, some clearly nativist and exclusionary, in these data? One possible explanation is that lifelong southerners have responded with a cultural backlash because the region is now subject to unparalleled, seemingly escalating immigration from Latin America. Such a rapid demographic transition—one, moreover, very much still underway—can be quite disorienting, threatening, no doubt, to those still in the region who came of age in a South etched in black and white, one in which orthodox Protestantism reigned unchallenged, and English, for most, was the only linguistic currency. During the 1990s, for example, among the six states with the highest growth rate of Hispanics, four were southern: Arkansas (#1), North Carolina (#3), Georgia (#4), and Tennessee (#6). Today, Latinos permeate parts of the region: the Atlanta metropolitan area was, in 2005, home to over 400,000 Latinos; Charlotte, to 112,000 Hispanics; New Orleans, 65,000; North Carolina's Triangle area, over 110,000; Houston, almost 1.7 million. The South—even in its divergence from and historical opposition to "America"—has always been thought more American than America, the place where American excesses, whether good or bad, could be safely deposited, used or abused as needed, and then returned. We southerners wear our Americanism, and our patriotism, on our sleeve, proudly, as we will happily show any curious onlooker. Still, the question continues to haunt: are all of the above sufficient reasons to explain why so many of us in this region hang on so tenaciously to such a constricted, anti-creedal expression of American identity?[15]

NOTES

We thank Woody Beck, Peggy Hargis, Dave Shaw, and Harry Watson for their valuable comments on an earlier version of this article. Please direct comments to Larry Griffin at ljg@unc.edu.

1. James Cobb and William Steuck, eds., *Globalization and the American South* (University of Georgia Press, 2006); James Peacock, Harry Watson, and Carrie Matthews, eds., *The American South in a Global World* (University of North Carolina Press, 2006); Carl Degler, "The Foundations of Southern Distinctiveness," *The Southern Review* 13 (Spring 1977): 225–39; Milton M. Gordon, *Assimilation in American Life: The Role of Race, Religion, and National Origins* (Oxford University Press, 1964); Arthur Mann, "From Immigration to Acculturation," in *Making America: The Society and Culture of the United States*, ed. Luther Luedtke (University of North Carolina Press, 1992), 68–80. The quote that serves as the title of this essay is from a statement by an undocumented Latino whose legal claim to American citizenship was delayed by the Immigration and Naturalization Service. It continues: "I'm No Longer One of 'Them.' I'm One of 'Us.'" *The Herald* (Rock Hill, S.C.), 4 July 1999.

2. The General Social Survey is widely used in public opinion studies and is fielded by the National Opinion Research Center at the University of Chicago (see http://www.norc.org/projects/General+Social+Survey.htm). The GSS consists of face-to-face interviews with a nationally representative sample of adults eighteen and older.

3. Mann, "From Immigration to Acculturation," 68. See, also, Michael Walzer, "What Does It Mean to Be An 'American'?" *Social Research* 57 (Fall 1990): 591–614.

4. W. B. Gallie, "Essentially Contested Concepts," in W. B. Gallie, *Philosophy and the Historical Understanding* (Schocken, 1964), 157–91; Gunnar Myrdal, *An American Dilemma: The Negro Problem and Modern Democracy* (Harper and Brothers, 1944), 4.

5. Myrdal, *An American Dilemma*, 5; Mann, "From Immigration to Acculturation," 70.

6. Theodore H. White, *The Making of the President, 1960* (Atheneum Publishers, 1961), 295. Kennedy's Houston speech is reprinted on pages 437–39.

7. On Fordice, see *The Washington Post*, 18 November 1992. On Moore, see *The New York Times*, 19 November 2002; 7 March 2004. Samuel Huntington, *Who Are We? The Challenges to America's National Identity* (Simon and Schuster, 2004). See, also, Alan Wolfe's review of Huntington, "Native Son: Samuel Huntington Defends the Homeland," *Foreign Affairs* 83.3 (May–June, 2004), 120. On Lamar Alexander, see Bloomberg at http://www.bloomberg. com/apps/news?pid=10000103&sid+a_LjjNFU9gBY&refer=us.

8. Wolfe, "Native Son," 121. Immigrants from Mexico alone account for half of the recent immigrants into the United States and compose almost 30 percent of the nation's foreign-born population. See Michael B. Katz, Mark J. Stern, and Jamie J. Fader, "The Mexican Immigration Debate: The View from History," *Social Science History* 31 (Summer 2007): 157–89. See, also, George Sánchez, "Face the Nation: Race, Immigration, and the Rise of Nativism in Late Twentieth Century America," *International Migration Review* 31 (Winter 1997): 1009–1030.

9. We lack information on the continuous residential histories of the GSS respondents. "Lifelong" southerners and "lifelong" nonsoutherners therefore are defined to be those who both lived in the South/Non-South at age sixteen and did so at the time of the survey.

10. See, for example, the report, "The Status of Muslim Civil Rights in the United States, 2002," from the Council on American-Islamic Relations, http://www.cair-net.org/civilrights2002/, accessed 29 May 2007.

11. John Egerton, *The Americanization of Dixie, the Southernization of America* (Harper's Magazine Press, 1974); Peter Applebome, *Dixie Rising: How the South is Shaping American Values, Politics, and Culture* (Times Books, 1996).

12. Both black and white lifelong southerners espouse more restrictive criteria than do their same-race peers in the other two regional groups, though the pattern is more pronounced for African Americans. Also, these black southerners generally are more particularistic than lifelong white southerners.

13. Again, this pattern holds for both black and white southerners.

14. In 2006, much fewer of the South's lifelong African Americans (49 percent) preferred a decrease in the number of immigrants than did whites who had resided in the region their whole life (71 percent). The region's African Americans were also both more supportive of granting ethnoracial minorities assistance from the state and less supportive of exclusionary policies toward the undocumented. Regional differences in most of the patterns in Tables 1 and 2 are only slightly dampened when we limit the analysis to native-born Americans. Foreign-born citizens are much less likely to tie "true Americanism" to attributes grounded in American birth or ancestry and, not surprisingly, are both considerably more positive in their assessment of immigrants and less exclusionary in their opinions about immigration policy.

15. For state-level statistics on Latinos, see U.S. Census Bureau at http://quickfacts.census. gov/qfd/, accessed 23 July 2007. Data are from the 2005 American Community Survey, conducted by the U.S. Census Bureau at http://factfinder.census.gov/home/saff/main.html?_lang=en, accessed 15 May 2007.

There's a Word for It—
The Origins of "Barbecue"

BY JOHN SHELTON REED

A French expedition to Florida in the 1560s included an artist, Jacques Le Moyne, one of whose sketches (here) of Timucua Indian life shows a mixed grill of alligators, snakes, and some kind of wildcat.

What could be more southern than barbecue? Even when entrepreneurs have taken the dish to other parts of the world, the names of their establishments pay tribute to the origins of their product, either explicitly (Memphis Championship Barbecue in Las Vegas, Memphis Minnie's in San Francisco, the Carolina Country Kitchen in Brooklyn, the Arkansas Café in London) or at least by implication (Jake and Earl's in Cambridge, Massachusetts, Daisy May's in Manhattan, Dixie's in Bellevue, Washington). Rivaled only by grits as the national dish of the South, barbecue would appear to be as southern, as indigenous, as it comes.

But, for all that southerners have made barbecue our own, the fact remains that this symbol of the South, like kudzu, is an import. The technique of cooking over hardwood coals or a low fire, or with smoke and indirect heat from hardwood, at a low temperature (about the boiling point of water) exists in a great many different cultures, and has from time immemorial: Europeans and Africans were both familiar with it before they arrived in the New World and found the native Indians doing it. The hogs and cattle that are the usual subjects of the enterprise were brought from Europe, as was the vinegar that goes into most sauces. The peppers that usually go in as well are a West Indian contribution. And tomatoes—well, that's a long story, but let's just say that they weren't grown and eaten in colonial North America.

Even the word *barbecue* seems to have been imported, although it underwent some changes after it was naturalized in Great Britain's southern colonies. The word came into English only some five hundred years ago. In the first decades of the 1500s Spanish explorers in the Caribbean found the locals using frameworks of sticks to support meat over fires. They did this either to slow-cook it or to cure and preserve it—as we do with country hams and jerky today—which one depends on the heat of the fire and the height of the framework. Both on the island of Hispaniola (modern-day Haiti and the Dominican Republic) and on the northern coast of South America this apparatus was called something that the Spanish heard as *barbacòa*, which soon became a Spanish word—one that is making its way into the South these days, via Mexico. A French expedition to Florida in the 1560s included an artist, Jacques Le Moyne, one of whose sketches of Timucua Indian life shows a mixed grill of alligators, snakes, and some kind of wildcat on just such a frame. The native Floridians also had a word like *barbacòa* for this rig, and indeed for all sorts of wooden structures, including watchtowers and raised sleeping platforms.

Some twenty years later, in 1585, Sir Walter Raleigh sent some folks to look things over on the coast of what would later be North Carolina. One member of that party was John White, "Gentleman of London," who later became governor

Barbe a Queue

One popular theory derives the word *barbecue* from the French "*barbe à queue*"—beard to tail—a nod to the practice of roasting whole hogs. This "absurd conjecture" (as the *Oxford English Dictionary* calls it) seems to have originated in 1829, when the *National Intelligencer* newspaper called supporters of Andrew Jackson "Barbacues," because they were "going the whole hog, from the beard *barbe* to the *queue* tail." Some apparently mistook this pun for a proposed derivation—the *Salem* (Massachusetts) *Gazette*, for example, which remarked that it was one that "we do not recollect to have ever heard of before, but which has every appearance of being the true one." This specious theory caught on, and has been endlessly repeated since.

The Q Factor

In colonial America and the early days of the Republic people spelled "barbecue" however they pleased. But the *–cue* spelling preferred by dictionary writers from Samuel Johnson (1755) to Noah Webster (1828) eventually became the standard. These days it is used roughly three times as often in the United States as a whole (and in Australia) as *barbeque*, the next most frequent spelling.

But not in the South. Despite the shortcomings of *barbeque* (it looks as if it should be pronounced "bar-beck," and one dictionary huffily points out that no other word in English has *que* as a stand-alone last syllable) it is in a statistical dead heat with barbe*cue* in the Carolinas, and over the mountains in Kentucky, Tennessee, Alabama, Mississippi, and Arkansas it's about twice as common as the authorized spelling. Throw in bar-b-que, bar-b-q, bbq, and so forth, and it's clear that Southerners really like that letter Q.

One of the few who has written about this is former Black Panther Bobby Seale, who finds the "Q" spellings more soulful; to him *–cue* represents "something drab, or even 'square,' as we used to say in the 1950s." It could also be that southerners don't like Yankees telling us how to spell our national dish. But I suspect that folks just like the way the letter recapitulates the sound of that last syllable. And why not?

Consider the mystic trigrammaton, BBQ. It is not in itself a word. Nor is it an acronym. It is rarely sounded out, like TVA, NBC, or BBC (the British Broadcasting Corporation). Usually it is pronounced "barbecue," just as *Xmas* is pronounced "Christmas." Which means that, linguistically speaking, it is an abbreviation.

But where did it come from? And why BBQ, rather than BBC? I haven't found an example of "BBQ" from before the twentieth century, so it's possible that it abbreviates the spelling barbe*que*, which is older. More likely, however, is that it abbreviates the *sound* of "barbecue," rather than its spelling—perhaps a predictable development in a culture where literacy has been a little shaky. It may be significant that it seems to have come into use only after there were barbecue stands whose owners needed signs to say what they were selling.

Some have asserted that "BBQ" comes from combination beer joints and pool halls that wanted to advertise "Bar, Beer, and Cues." I mention this ridiculous theory only for the sake of thoroughness.

of the ill-fated Roanoke Island colony (and grandfather of Virginia Dare who was, as every North Carolina schoolchild once knew, the first English child born in North America). White made sketches of what he saw, including Croatan Indians "broyling their fishe over the flame—they took great heed that they bee not burntt." Unfortunately, he didn't say what the indigenous Tar Heels called their cooker, but whatever they called it, it's obviously a *barbacòa*, too.

William Dampier, naturalist and sometime pirate, wrote in 1697 about a visit to some West Indians when he and his companions "lay there all night, upon our Borbecu's, or frames of Sticks, raised about 3 foot from the Ground." Yankees and Australians who talk about putting meat "on the barbecue" can appeal to Dampier for precedent, but in colonial North America and England, as in the South today, the word usually referred to a process of cooking or to what was cooked, rather than to the frame on which it was done.

The earliest use of the English word that I've encountered comes from 1661, when Edmund Hickeringill's *Jamaica Viewed* reported that animals "are slain, And their flesh forthwith Barbacu'd and eat," but by 1689 in a play called *THE Widdow Ranter OR, The HISTORY of Bacon in Virginia*, "the rabble" fixing to lynch one Colonel Wellman cry, "Let's barbicu this fat rogue." That the word could be used casually on the stage shows that by then it must have been familiar to London audiences. (The play was written by the remarkable Aphra Behn, the first Englishwoman to be a professional writer, and "Bacon" in the title refers to the leader of Bacon's Rebellion of 1676, not to side meat.) About the same time, the Boston Puritan Cotton Mather used the word in the same gruesome sense when he reported that several hundred Narragansetts slaughtered by New England troops in 1675 (among them women, children, and elders burned in their lodges) had been "terribly Barbikew'd."

A few years later John Lawson, surveyor-general of North Carolina, also used the word without explanation. In his *New Voyage to Carolina* (1709) Lawson encountered "barbakued"—that is, smoked and dried—venison, fish, and even peaches. Some Santee Indians served him "fat barbacu'd Venison" that sounds like a sort of jerky: "the Woman of the Cabin took [it] and tore in Pieces with her Teeth"—pulled, not sliced—"so put it into a Mortar, beating it into Rags," then boiled it. But he was also served "roasted or barbakued Turkey, eaten with Bears Fat." Not long after that, the physician and naturalist John Brickell gave a very similar account (so similar in fact that it may have been plagiarized) in his *Natural History of North Carolina* (1737).

The one suggestion I've found that the English word was *not* taken from the Spanish version of a Caribbean Indian word comes from Robert Beverly's *History and Present State of Virginia* (1705). Beverly reported that the Indians of the Carolinas and Virginia had "two ways of Broyling viz. one by laying the Meat itself upon

By *1689 in a play called* THE Widdow Ranter OR, The HISTORY *of Bacon in Virginia, "the rabble" fixing to lynch one Colonel Wellman cry, "Let's barbicu this fat rogue." That the word could be used casually on the stage shows that by then it must have been familiar to London audiences. The play was written by the remarkable Aphra Behn (here), the first Englishwoman to be a professional writer, and "Bacon" in the title refers to the leader of Bacon's Rebellion of 1676, not to side meat.*

the Coals, the other by laying it upon Sticks rais'd upon Forks at some distance above the live Coals, which heats more gently, and drys up the Gravy"; this latter, he added, "they, and we also from them, call Barbacueing." (Whether they had the same word as their Caribbean cousins or not, they plainly got the grilling versus barbecuing thing.)

The English may have copied the Indians' vocabulary, but they didn't feel constrained to copy their stone-age gear. Anglo-Saxons and Celts had been roasting meat for a few thousand years themselves and had made a few improvements in the matter of cooking frames. In 1732 Richard Bradley, in *The Country Housewife*, gave directions for "an Hog barbecued": "Take a large Grid-iron, with two or three Ribs in it, and set it upon a stand of iron, about three Foot and a half high, and upon that, lay your Hog, . . . Belly-side downwards." And a 1744 advertisement in the Boston *News-Letter* offered for sale "A Lusty Negro Man, works well at the Smith's Trade; likewise a Grate for to burn Coal; a large Gridiron, fit for a large Kitchen, or a Barbeque." It also offers the earliest example I've found of the *–que* spelling, although spelling was so random at the time that it hardly signifies.

Still, the process of cooking or smoking meat on some sort of frame remained identified with the Indians. When Colonel George Washington, trying to get provisions for his troops during the French and Indian War, wrote his superior officer in 1758, "We have not an ounce of salt provision of any kind here; and it is impossible to preserve the fresh (especially as we have no Salt) by any other means than barbacuing it in the indian manner," he was evidently writing about smoking meat to cure it, not to cook it. Later, however, the future Father of His Country often wrote about going to "barbecues" where cooking was the object:

The Three Pigs of Peckham

Barbecue historian Robert Moss finds the first detailed account of an Anglo-American barbecue in a travel account published in 1707 by an Englishman named Edward Ward. In *The Barbacue Feast:, or the Three Pigs of Peckham, Broiled Under an Apple Tree*, Ward reported that the white folks of Peckham, Jamaica, had "their English appetites so deprav'd and vitiated" by rum that they desired "a Litter of Pigs nicely cook'd after the West Indian manner." Three hogs were placed on a wooden frame over coals, and "the best part of the town of Peckham" turned out to watch and to eat, "expressing as much Joy in the Looks and Actions, as a Gang of wild *Cannibals* who, when they have taken a Stranger, first dance round him, and afterwards devour him."

This was whole-hog cooking: "According to the *Indian* fashion, they made no Diminution of the Creatures, but in taking out their Intrails, for broiling, they lay, with their Heads, Tails, Pettitoes [trotters], and Hoofs on, to the Amazement of the Crowd, and the Honour of the Cook." "A most admirable Composition of Green *Virginia* Pepper and *Madeira* wine" was "plentifully daubed on with a Fox's Tail ty'd onto a stick," then the hogs were placed on a log and quartered with an ax. The meat was judged "Incomparable Food, fit for the table of a *Sagamoor* [Indian chief]."

for example, "Went in to Alexandria to a Barbecue and stayed all Night" (1769), "Went to a Barbicue of my own giving at Accotinck" (1773), "Went to the Barbacue at Accatinck" (1774). (Notice that his spelling was as independent as his subsequent politics.)

Washington's use of *barbecue* to refer to a social event was not unusual: That use of the word dates from at least 1733, although it was apparently an Americanism. When a young Virginian wrote to a London friend in 1784 that he was "continually at Balls & Barbecues," he added, "the latter I don't suppose you know what I mean" and went on to explain: "it's a shoat & sometimes a Lamb or Mutton & indeed sometimes a Beef splitt into & stuck on spitts, & then they have a large Hole dugg in the ground where they have a number of Coals made of the Bark [?] of Trees, put in this Hole. & then they lay the Meat over that within about six inches of the Coals, & then they Keep basting it with Butter & Salt & Water & turning it every now and then, until it is done, we then dine under a large shady tree or an harbour made of green bushes, under which we have benches & seats to sit on when we dine sumptuously."

This was the kind of thing the itinerant Anglican parson Charles Woodmason probably smelled, roaming the South Carolina backcountry in 1768, when he wrote in his journal: "I had last Week Experience of the Velocity and force of the Air—By smelling a Barbicu dressing in the Woods upwards of six Miles," and it sounds pretty nice, if you get to sit under the "harbour." Less so, of course, if you're a slave on the digging and basting crew.

Even though the word had been naturalized in the thirteen colonies, the British continued to see it as West Indian. Also, most references at this time were to whole hogs (or whole other animals) being cooked—the practice in the Caribbean and, now as then, in eastern North Carolina. When the poet Alexander Pope wrote in 1733 that a man named Oldfield, who was famous for his appetite, "Cries, 'Send me, Gods! a whole Hog barbecu'd!'" he added a note for his English readers explaining that "a whole hog barbecu'd" was "a *West-Indian* Term of Gluttony, a Hog roasted whole, stu'd with Spice, and basted with *Madera* Wine."

When news of the end of the Revolutionary War reached New Bern, North Carolina, in June of 1783, a Venezuelan-born Spanish army officer named Francisco de Miranda was in town. He wrote later: "By way of celebration for this event, starting at one o'clock, there was a barbecue (a roast pig) and a barrel of rum, from which the leading officials and citizens of the region promiscuously ate and drank with the meanest and lowest kind of people, holding hands and drinking from the same cup. It is impossible to imagine, without seeing it, a more purely democratic gathering. . . . There were some drunks, some friendly fisticuffs, and one man was injured."

Just so, Samuel Johnson's famous *Dictionary* (1755) defined the verb *to barbecue* as "a term used in the West-Indies for dressing a hog whole; which, being split to the backbone, is laid flat upon a large gridiron, raised about two feet above a charcoal fire, with which it is surrounded" and *barbecue*, the noun, as "a hog drest whole in the West Indian manner." Virtually identical definitions, probably cribbed from Johnson, can be found in many, many subsequent dictionaries. In 1828 Noah Webster's *Dictionary of the American Language* also defined the word as, "in the West Indies, a hog roasted whole," but expanded the definition: "It is, with us [i.e., Americans], used for an ox or perhaps any other animal dressed in like manner."

Webster was from Connecticut, but an 1816 *Vocabulary, or, Collection of words and phrases, which have been supposed to be peculiar to the United States of America* [etc.] had given the first indication that barbecue was becoming a southern thing. Quoting an English source from 1798, it said that barbecue was "a porket . . . stuffed with spices and other rich ingredients, and basted with Madeira wine," then added, "*Used in the* Southern *states*" (although "not peculiar to the *United States*; it is used in the *West Indies* also").

Notice that these dictionaries show the emergence of yet another use of this

versatile word: *a barbecue* could mean the critter being barbecued—and not just a hog. In 1796 Hugh Henry Brackenridge wrote a humorous reply to a challenge to duel, which read in part, "I do not see any good it would do me to put a bullet through any part of your body. . . . You might make a good barbecue, it is true, being of the nature of a raccoon or an opossum; but people are not in the habit of barbecuing anything human now."

So by the mid-1700s we had *barbecue* as a kind of equipment for a style of cooking called *barbecuing*, and we had *barbecue* as an event of the sort that George Washington and his contemporaries went to, and we had *barbecue* as a word for the subject of the undertaking—pig, ox, shad, whatever (although this last use seems to have disappeared). But we apparently did not yet have *barbecue* as the point of all this: the dish prepared on a barbecue-device and served at a barbecue-event, what a barbecue-creature becomes after it is barbecue-processed. When did barbecued pork become *barbecue*?

Someone may come up with an earlier example, but the earliest I've found comes from 1808. Oddly enough, it comes from a Yankee—although he was disparaging southern folkways at the time. In a speech on the floor of Congress, Representative Josiah Quincy of Boston denounced the kind of partisan stump speech commonly delivered "in this quarter of the country . . . while the gin circulated, while barbecue was roasting." (It was a southern thing. He didn't understand.)

By the middle of the nineteenth century this use of the word was increasingly common in print, especially in southern newspapers, usually in the context of political rallies. In 1859, for instance, the *Weekly Standard* of Raleigh wrote that one politician's "constituents had been bought up by whiskey and barbecue." The next year, the same paper wrote of a gathering in Shelby, "The barbecue was excellent. Not a Douglas man was found upon the ground." In 1868 the *Petersburg Index* reported that the three thousand Democrats at a rally in Nash County, North Carolina, "marched to the grove, near by, where a bountiful supply of barbecue, vegetables, etc., etc., refreshed the 'inner man,' and to which ample justice was done."

True, as late as 1894, when the Statesville (North Carolina) *Landmark* wrote of an occasion where "several hundred ladies were present, and the contents of their baskets, supplemented by 'barbecue' from the committee, composed the repast," the paper put the noun in quotation marks, suggesting that the usage remained colloquial. Still, by then everyone seems to have known that it meant something you could put on a plate or a sandwich.

As early as 1676 a Quaker named Humphrey Griffin purchased land near "Barbicue" Swamp in what is now Hertford County in the far northeastern part of North Carolina. Where the swamp got its name is not known, but historian William S. Powell reports that another North Carolina Barbecue Swamp, in Harnett County, was named by the early Gaelic-speaking settler Niall Ruadh, or Red Neill McNeill. When he first saw it, about 1750, the mist rising from it reminded him of the smoke from barbecue pits he had seen in the West Indies. Barbecue Presbyterian Church, organized in 1758, became the mother church for the many Scottish Presbyterian churches in this area. (Flora MacDonald worshipped there.) The church still serves Harnett County's Barbecue Township.

Only after that was understood was the way open to argue about what barbecue *is*. But that's another long story.

NOTE

This essay was adapted from *Holy Smoke*, by John Shelton Reed, Dale Volberg Reed, and Will McKinney, to be published in 2008 by the University of North Carolina Press.

About the Contributors

Carl L. Bankston III is professor and chair in the Department of Sociology and co-director of the Asian Studies program at Tulane University. He is author or editor of fourteen books, which have received numerous noteworthy awards, and he has published over 100 articles or book chapters. He is the current president of the Mid-South Sociological Association.

Peter A. Coclanis is Albert R. Newsome Professor of History and associate provost for International Affairs at UNC-Chapel Hill. He is the author of many works in southern and international economic history. His most recent book is *Time's Arrow, Time's Cycle: Globalization in Southeast Asia over la Longue Durée*.

Nan Enstad is associate professor of history at the University of Wisconsin, Madison, and the author of *Ladies of Labor, Girls of Adventure: Working Women, Popular Culture and Labor Politics*. She is currently writing a book tentatively titled, *The Jim Crow Cigarette: Following Tobacco Road from North Carolina to China and Back*.

Lisa Eveleigh spent her salad days working—and eating—in Bill Smith's kitchen at Restaurant La Résidence, in Chapel Hill, North Carolina, before becoming managing editor of *Southern Cultures*.

Larry J. Griffin, with Harry Watson, edits *Southern Cultures* and is the Reed Professor of Sociology at the University of North Carolina at Chapel Hill, where he also teaches in the history and American Studies departments. His teaching and research interests include collective memory, social identity, and the intersection of race, rights, and region.

Louis M. Kyriakoudes is an associate professor of history at the University of Southern Mississippi. He is the author of "The Grand Ole Opry and Big Tobacco: Radio Scripts from the Files of the R. J. Reynolds Tobacco Company, 1948 to 1959," published in the Summer 2006 *Southern Cultures*. He is currently writing a history of cigarette smoking.

Rebecca Lilly holds a Ph.D. in philosophy from Princeton University, and an M.F.A. in creative writing from Cornell University. She has published two books on spiritual practice and two collections of poems: *You Want to Sell Me a Small Antique*, which won the Peregrine Smith Poetry Prize, and *Shadwell Hills*, a book of haiku.

Marko Maunula is an assistant professor of history at Clayton State University. A Finnish journalist in his previous life, his academic interests now focus on the South's interaction with the world. He enjoys East Carolina barbecue, Tar Heel basketball, and Georgia football.

Katherine McFarland is a graduate student in sociology at the University of North Carolina at Chapel Hill. A new transplant to the South, she is busy pursuing all aspects of southern culture.

Tore C. Olsson is a Ph.D. candidate in history at the University of Georgia. Though born in Sweden and raised in Boston, he is fascinated with southern history and how recent immigration has transformed the region.

John Shelton Reed is spending the fall semester of 2007 as Mark Clark Visiting Professor at the Citadel, where he is also a lieutenant colonel in the Unorganized Militia of South Carolina. He says that he now realizes that he had waited all his life to have students salute him.

John Russell is a writer, businessman, and lawyer who has worked extensively in economic development in both the policy and corporate arenas, first in the venture capital industry and currently in pharmaceuticals. He serves as executive vice president for government affairs and health policy for Quintiles Transnational Corp. and has written and lectured in North America, Europe, and Asia on economics and health policy issues. His novel, *Favorite Sons*, won the Sir Walter Raleigh Award in 1993.

The Special Global South Issue's DVD

Neighborhood Voices
New Immigrants in Northeast Central Durham, North Carolina

Located inside the back cover.

INTRODUCTION

In 1998 UNC-Chapel Hill's Southern Oral History Program (SOHP) launched "Listening for a Change: North Carolina Communities in Transition," a major oral history research initiative that examined the profound demographic, racial, economic, environmental, agricultural, and other transformations that have reshaped North Carolina and its communities since World War II. "Listening for a Change" was designed to capture the voices and preserve the insights of those people whose life experiences are not typically reflected in historical accounts. These "ordinary" women and men — working people, black, brown, red, yellow, and white, old and young, longtime state residents and new arrivals — graciously shared their extraordinary stories with interviewers from the SOHP. *Neighborhood Voices*, one of ten "Listening for a Change" component projects, explores the impact of rapid Latino immigration into the Northeast Central Durham neighborhood, long ago a mostly white area and for many decades a predominantly African-American community. Using sound, photographs, and video, the *Neighborhood Voices* DVD presents a compelling portrait of the community's past and present. We hope that *Neighborhood Voices*, conceived and conducted in close collaboration with members of the community, will encourage the conversation and bridge-building through which neighbors continue to strengthen Northeast Central Durham.

The *Neighborhood Voices* project was made possible by a major grant from the Z. Smith Reynolds Foundation and additional support from the Carolina Center for Public Service at UNC-Chapel Hill and the UNC Institute on Aging. *Neighborhood Voices/Voces del Barrio* received additional support from the North Carolina Humanities Council, the UNC Center for the Study of the American South, and the Harold S. and Dorothy Bean Conrad Oral History Endowment.

USING THE *NEIGHBORHOOD VOICES* DVD

The presentation opens with an introduction comprised of several automated screens, and the presentation's content appears in three main chapters. "Durham History" chronicles Northeast Central Durham from the 1850s through the 1990s. "New Immigrants" describes the experiences of Latino immigrants, whose numbers have increased dramatically since the early 1990s. "Future Visions" explores the challenges confronting African Americans and their new Latino neighbors as they struggle to forge mutually satisfactory approaches to life in their vibrant, bicultural community.

The DVD is bilingual. Audio excerpts are accompanied by subtitles in the second language, making the DVD useful as a language instruction tool.

CREDITS

Neighborhood Voices was conceived and executed by Ted Richardson, with design and production assistance from Archana Gowda and Paige West.

Edited and written by Ted Richardson, after the work of Jill Hemming, Alicia Rouverol, and Angela Hornsby.

Photography and video by Ted Richardson. Historical photographs courtesy of the Durham Public Library and the Hayti Heritage Center in Durham, North Carolina.

DVD *mastering by* Archana Gowda and Rob Roberts.

This DVD is a multimedia extension of the Southern Oral History Program's "Neighborhood Voices/Voces del Barrio" research project, which was directed by SOHP research associates Alicia Rouverol and Jill Hemming.

Research Project staff and advisors: Katushka Olavé, Jacqueline Wagstaff, Luis Alvarenga, Ruby Mason, Will Atwater, and Debra Davis.

Interviewers: Ciro Arroyo-Vincenté, Colin Austin, Jill Hemming, Angela Hornsby, Ann Kaplan, Katushka Olavé, Alicia Rouverol, and Ted Richardson.

Translations: Míriam Granado, Katushka Olavé, Claudio Fuentes, Colin Austin, Ted Richardson, and Victoria Moxey.

El DVD sobre el Especial del Sur Global

Voces del Barrio

Nuevos Inmigrantes en la zona Noreste del Centro de Durham,
Carolina del Norte

Situado en el interior.

INTRODUCCIÓN

En 1998 el Programa de Historia Oral (SOHP) de
la Universidad de Carolina del Norte lanzó "Escuchando el Cambio: Las comunidades de Carolina
del Norte en Transición," una iniciativa de investigación que examinó las profundas transformaciones
demográficas, raciales, económicas, ambientales,
agrícolas y de otros tipos que han dado nueva forma
a Carolina del Norte y sus comunidades desde la
segunda guerra mundial. "Escuchando el Cambio"
ha captado las voces y preservado las impresiones de
la gente cuyas experiencias de toda una vida no son
típicamente reflejadas en registros históricos. Estos
hombres y mujeres "corrientes" —gente trabajadora,
gente que ha vivido en el estado mucho tiempo, vie-
jos y jovenes, de piel negra, morena, roja, amarilla y
blanca, y los recién llegados— amablemente compar-
tieron sus historias con entrevistadores del SOHP.

Voces del Barrio, uno de los diez componentes del
proyecto "Escuchando el Cambio," ha explorado el
impacto de la rápida inmigración latina en el noreste
del centro de Durham, que hace mucho tiempo
era un barrio habitado principalmente por blancos
y luego por muchas décadas una comunidad pre-
dominantemente afro-americana. Utilizando sonido,
fotografías y vídeo, el DVD *Voces del Barrio* presenta
un convincente retrato del presente y el pasado de
la comunidad. Esperamos que *Voces del Barrio* que el
SOHP ha concebido y dirigido en estrecha colabo-
ración con los miembros de la comunidad, animará
las conversaciones y el tendido de puentes a través
los cuales los vecinos siguen fortaleciendo el noreste
del centro de Durham.

La iniciativa "Escuchando el Cambio: Las Comunidades en Carolina del Norte en Transición" del
programa de historia oral fue posible gracias a una
importante subvención de la fundación Z. Smith
Reynolds y adicional apoyo financiero del Centro de
Servicios Públicos de Carolina y el Instituto de En-
vejecimiento de UNC. *Voces del Barrio* también recibió
apoyo del Consejo de Humanidades de Carolina del
Norte, el Centro de estudios sureños americanos
de UNC y la beca para Historia Oral de Harold S. y
Dorothy Bean Conrad.

UTILIZACIÓN EL DVD *VOCES DEL BARRIO*

El DVD comienza con una introducción constitu-
ida por varias pantallas automáticas. El contenido del
DVD aparece dividido en tres secciones principales.
"Historia de Durham" relata el pasado del noreste
del centro Durham desde la década de 1850 hasta la
de 1990. "Nuevos Inmigrantes" describe las experiencias de los inmigrantes latinos recién llegados
cuya población ha aumentado rápidamente desde el
principio de los años noventa. "Visiones de Futuro"
explora los desafíos que enfrentan a los afro-ameri-
canos y a sus nuevos vecinos latinos mientras luchan
para forjar enfoques mutuamente satisfactorios a la
vida en su vibrante comunidad bicultural.

El DVD es bilingüe. Las reproducciones de audio
de las entrevistas de la historia oral están acompa-
ñadas por una traducción en pantalla en el segundo
idioma, lo que convierte el DVD en una herramienta
ideal para la enseñanza del lenguaje.

CRÉDITOS

Voces del Barrio fue concebido y llevado a cabo por
Ted Richardson con la ayuda en el diseño y producción de Archana Gowda y Paige West.

Editado y escrito por Ted Richardson, Jill Hemming,
Alicia Rouverol, y Angela Hornsby.

Fotografía y vídeo por Ted Richardson, Durham
Public Library, y Hayti Heritage Center.

Producción del DVD por Archana Gowda y Rob
Roberts.

El DVD es una extensión en formato multi-media
del "Neighborhood Voices/Voces del Barrio" del
proyecto de investigación del Programa de Historia
Oral Sureña que fue dirigido por los investigadores
asociados del SOHP, Jill Henning y Alicia Rouverol.

Personal del proyecto y consejeros: Katushka Olavé,
Jacqueline Wagstaff, Luis Alvarenga, Ruby Mason,
Will Atwater, y Debra Davis.

Entrevistadores: Ciro Arroyo-Vincenté, Colin Austin, Jill Hemming, Angela Hornsby, Ann Kaplan, Katushka Olavé, Alicia Rouverol, y Ted Richardson.

Traducciónes: Míriam Granado, Katushka Olavé,
Claudio Fuentes, Colin Austin, Ted Richardson, y
Victoria Moxey.

UNC
CENTER FOR THE STUDY
OF THE AMERICAN SOUTH

POSTDOCTORAL FELLOWSHIPS IN SOUTHERN STUDIES

The UNC Center for the Study of the American South invites applications for two one-year postdoctoral fellowships in the history, culture, or society of the American South, to begin July 1, 2008. The awards support two outstanding junior scholars in the revision of book-length manuscripts for publication in fields related to the South, broadly construed to include the states of the former Confederacy and adjoining areas. Applications are welcome from any field, but projects are especially welcome that draw on the special collections of the UNC-CH Library or other research collections of the Triangle area, or explicitly engage issues of southern regional identity or distinctiveness.

Support. Each Fellowship provides a salary of $40,000, plus health insurance and $3,000 in research and travel funds. Fellows may arrange to teach no more than one course at UNC during the fellowship term.

Requirements. Applicants must have received the Ph.D. prior to the beginning of the fellowship year and no more than four years before the year begins. Scholars who have received tenure, published a previous scholarly book, or signed a book publication contract are not be eligible.

Publication. Fellows submit their manuscripts to UNC Press. Acceptance is contingent on peer review and the editors' discretion, and all manuscripts are subject to UNC Press's editorial processes.

Applications. Applications are due January 9, 2008, and consist of a cover sheet (available at *www.unc.edu/depts/csas/*), curriculum vitae, three letters of recommendation, a three- to five-page description of the project, including a comprehensive plan for revision of an existing manuscript, and a sample of writing from the project of no more than thirty pages. Following selection, each Fellow must submit a hard copy of the dissertation or existing manuscript.

Postdoctoral Fellowships in Southern Studies
The Center for the Study of the American South
410 East Franklin Street, CB# 9127, UNC-CH
Chapel Hill, NC 27599-9127

919-962-5665, South@unc.edu, or *www.unc.edu/depts/csas* for more info.

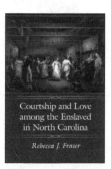

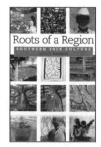

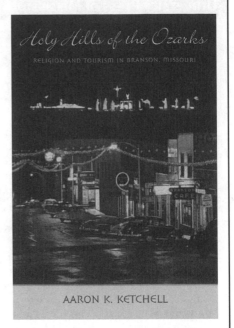

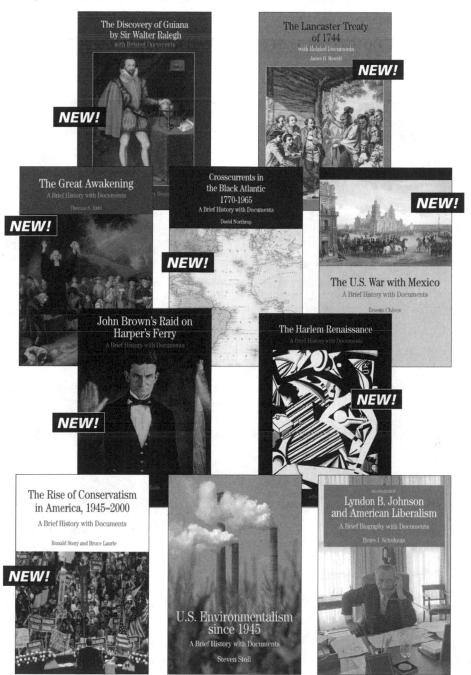

SAVE the DATE

Beyond the Sunbelt:
Southern Economic Development in a Global Context

APRIL 13 - 14, 2008

The University of North Carolina at Chapel Hill is pleased to announce its annual interdisciplinary conference on the globalization of the southern United States. This year's conference - the fourth in the series *Navigating the Global American South* - will bring together 200 academics, policy makers, and economic development practicioners from across the region and beyond. A collaboration of the Center for Global Initiatives, the Center for the Study of the American South, and the Office of Economic and Business Development, the goal is to examine how global forces are shaping regional economic development strategies and to consider the best paths forward.

For more information about the 2008 conference, or past conferences in the series, please visit:

globalsouth.unc.edu

UNC
GLOBAL

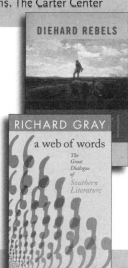
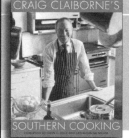

The Stories
and Music
of the South

Jesus in the Mist
Stories
Paul Ruffin
"The rural South of the 1960s is the setting of
Ruffin's stories, many of which feature characters
proud to be successful high school dropouts
with minimum-wage jobs. . . . Flawed, stubborn
characters pursuing their dreams and on a quest to
understand their purpose dominate these stories,
which paint a realistic picture of the social tensions
of the time."—*Library Journal*
208 pp., cloth, $24.95

Votaries of Apollo
*The St. Cecilia Society and the Patronage of
Concert Music in Charleston, South Carolina,
1766–1820*
Nicholas Michael Butler
Blending archival research with musical expertise,
Butler offers a definitive history of the dynamic
and vibrant concert life in Charleston, South
Carolina, during the era from 1766 to 1820, when
the exclusive St. Cecilia Society functioned as North
America's premier musical organization.
384 pp., 28 illus., cloth,$49.95
The Carolina Lowcountry and the Atlantic World

THE UNIVERSITY OF
SOUTH CAROLINA PRESS

Available at bookstores or call
800.768.2500
www.sc.edu/uscpress

UNITED STATES POSTAL SERVICE
Statement of Ownership, Management, and Circulation
(All Periodicals Publications Except Requester Publications)

1. Publication Title
Southern Cultures

2. Publication Number
1 0 6 8 - 8 2 1 8

3. Filing Date
September 24, 2007

4. Issue Frequency
quarterly (Spring, Summer, Fall, Winter)

5. Number of Issues Published Annually
4

6. Annual Subscription Price
$28 Individuals
$52.20 Institutions

7. Complete Mailing Address of Known Office of Publication *(Not printer) (Street, city, county, state, and ZIP+4®)*
Center for the Study of the American South, 410 East Franklin St,
CB#9127, UNC-CH, Chapel Hill, Orange County, NC 27599-9127

Contact Person
Suzi Waters

Telephone *(Include area code)*
919-962-4201

8. Complete Mailing Address of Headquarters or General Business Office of Publisher *(Not printer)*
The University of North Carolina Press, 116 South Boundary St,
Chapel Hill, Orange County, NC 27514

9. Full Names and Complete Mailing Addresses of Publisher, Editor, and Managing Editor *(Do not leave blank)*

Publisher *(Name and complete mailing address)*
The University of North Carolina Press, 116 South Boundary St,
Chapel Hill, Orange County, NC 27514

Editor *(Name and complete mailing address)*
Harry L Watson and Larry J Griffin, UNC Center for the Study of the American South, UNC-CH,
CB#9127, 410 E Franklin St, Chapel Hill, Orange County, NC 27599-9127

Managing Editor *(Name and complete mailing address)*
Dave Shaw, UNC Center for the Study of the American South, 410 E Franklin St, CB#9127,
UNC-CH, Chapel Hill, Orange County, NC 27599-9127

10. Owner *(Do not leave blank. If the publication is owned by a corporation, give the name and address of the corporation immediately followed by the names and addresses of all stockholders owning or holding 1 percent or more of the total amount of stock. If not owned by a corporation, give the names and addresses of the individual owners. If owned by a partnership or other unincorporated firm, give its name and address as well as those of each individual owner. If the publication is published by a nonprofit organization, give its name and address.)*

Full Name	Complete Mailing Address
The University of North Carolina at Chapel Hill	Chapel Hill, NC 27599

11. Known Bondholders, Mortgagees, and Other Security Holders Owning or Holding 1 Percent or More of Total Amount of Bonds, Mortgages, or Other Securities. If none, check box ► ☒ None

Full Name	Complete Mailing Address

12. Tax Status *(For completion by nonprofit organizations authorized to mail at nonprofit rates) (Check one)*
The purpose, function, and nonprofit status of this organization and the exempt status for federal income tax purposes:
☒ Has Not Changed During Preceding 12 Months
☐ Has Changed During Preceding 12 Months *(Publisher must submit explanation of change with this statement)*

PS Form **3526**, September 2006 *(Page 1 of 3 (Instructions Page 3))* PSN 7530-01-000-9931 PRIVACY NOTICE: See our privacy policy on www.usps.com

---

13. Publication Title
Southern Cultures

14. Issue Date for Circulation Data
Fall 2007, Vol 13#3 | September 6, 2007

15. Extent and Nature of Circulation

		Average No. Copies Each Issue During Preceding 12 Months	No. Copies of Single Issue Published Nearest to Filing Date
a. Total Number of Copies *(Net press run)*		3213	3450
b. Paid Circulation (By Mail and Outside the Mail)	(1) Mailed Outside-County Paid Subscriptions Stated on PS Form 3541 *(Include paid distribution above nominal rate, advertiser's proof copies, and exchange copies)*	2614	3057
	(2) Mailed In-County Paid Subscriptions Stated on PS Form 3541 *(Include paid distribution above nominal rate, advertiser's proof copies, and exchange copies)*		
	(3) Paid Distribution Outside the Mails Including Sales Through Dealers and Carriers, Street Vendors, Counter Sales, and Other Paid Distribution Outside USPS®		
	(4) Paid Distribution by Other Classes of Mail Through the USPS (e.g. First-Class Mail®)		
c. Total Paid Distribution *(Sum of 15b (1), (2),(3), and (4))*		2614	3057
d. Free or Nominal Rate Distribution (By Mail and Outside the Mail)	(1) Free or Nominal Rate Outside-County Copies Included on PS Form 3541	150	186
	(2) Free or Nominal Rate In-County Copies Included on PS Form 3541		
	(3) Free or Nominal Rate Copies Mailed at Other Classes Through the USPS (e.g. First-Class Mail)		
	(4) Free or Nominal Rate Distribution Outside the Mail *(Carriers or other means)*		
e. Total Free or Nominal Rate Distribution *(Sum of 15d (1), (2), (3), and (4))*		150	186
f. Total Distribution *(Sum of 15c and 15e)*		2764	3243
g. Copies not Distributed *(See Instructions to Publishers #4 (page #3))*		449	207
h. Total *(Sum of 15f and g)*		3213	3450
i. Percent Paid *(15c divided by 15f times 100)*		95%	94%

16. Publication of Statement of Ownership
☒ If the publication is a general publication, publication of this statement is required. Will be printed
in the **Winter 2007** issue of this publication. ☐ Publication not required.

17. Signature and Title of Editor, Publisher, Business Manager, or Owner
[signature] CFO, UNC PRESS

Date 9/24/07

I certify that all information furnished on this form is true and complete. I understand that anyone who furnishes false or misleading information on this form or who omits material or information requested on the form may be subject to criminal sanctions (including fines and imprisonment) and/or civil sanctions (including civil penalties).

PS Form **3526**, September 2006 *(Page 2 of 3)*